CW01371713

Paganism

Everything from Ancient, Hellenic, Norse, and Celtic Paganism to Heathenry, Wicca, and Other Modern Pagan Beliefs and Practices

© Copyright 2021

The contents of this book may not be reproduced, duplicated or transmitted without direct written permission from the author.

Under no circumstances will any legal responsibility or blame be held against the publisher for any reparation, damages, or monetary loss due to the information herein, either directly or indirectly.

Legal Notice:

This book is copyright protected. This is only for personal use. You cannot amend, distribute, sell, use, quote, or paraphrase any part of the content within this book without the consent of the author.

Disclaimer Notice:

Please note the information within this document is for educational and entertainment purposes only. Every attempt has been made to provide accurate, up-to-date, and reliable, complete information. No warranties of any kind are expressed or implied. Readers acknowledge that the author is not engaging in the rendering of legal, financial, medical, or professional advice. The content of this book has been derived from various sources. Please consult a licensed professional before attempting any techniques outlined in this book.

By reading this document, the reader agrees that under no circumstances is the author responsible for any losses, direct or indirect, which are incurred as a result of the use of information contained within this document, including, but not limited to, errors, omissions, or inaccuracies.

Your Free Gift (only available for a limited time)

Thanks for getting this book! If you want to learn more about various spirituality topics, then join Mari Silva's community and get a free guided meditation MP3 for awakening your third eye. This guided meditation mp3 is designed to open and strengthen ones third eye so you can experience a higher state of consciousness. Simply visit the link below the image to get started.

https://spiritualityspot.com/meditation

Contents

INTRODUCTION 1
CHAPTER 1: PAGANISM THROUGHOUT THE AGES 3
    THE MEANING OF PAGANISM..5
    HISTORY 7
    CLASSICAL ANTIQUITY 7
    LATE ANTIQUITY AND CHRISTIANIZATION..8
    PRE-ISLAMIC PAGANISM...8
    EARLY MODERN PAGANISM 9
    MODERN PAGANISM 10
CHAPTER 2: CORE BELIEFS OF PAGANISM..12
CHAPTER 3: HELLENIC AND ROMAN PAGANISM................................21
    GREEK RELIGION 22
    ROMAN RELIGION 27
    PAGAN OBJECT WORSHIP 27
CHAPTER 4: HEATHENRY, ASATRU, AND ODINISM 29
    MYTHS AND LEGENDS OF THE ASATRU 30
CHAPTER 5: CELTIC PAGANISM AND DRUIDRY 37
    FEATURES OF DRUIDRY 39
    GODS AND GODDESSES 43
    MODERN DRUIDRY 45

CHAPTER 6: HINDUISM AND MULTI-GOD FAITHS OF THE FAR EAST 46

Chinese Mythology 50
Japanese Mythology 52

CHAPTER 7: EGYPTIAN AND MIDDLE EASTERN PAGANISM 54

Creation Myth 55
Gods & Goddesses 57

CHAPTER 8: SLAVIC PAGANISM 62

Slavic Creation Myth 63
Deities 64
Modern Slavic Paganism 69

CHAPTER 9: INDIGENOUS PAGANISM: A SHAMANIC VIEW 70

Beliefs 71
Forms of Shamanism 72

CHAPTER 10: WICCA: A MODERN APPROACH 78

Wiccan Holidays 82

CHAPTER 11: AGNOSTIC PAGANISM & OTHER PATHS 87

History of Agnostic & Atheistic Paganism 87

CHAPTER 12: THE MODERN PAGAN: CHOOSE THE RIGHT PATH FOR YOU 94

Eclectic Paganism 97

CONCLUSION 103

HERE'S ANOTHER BOOK BY MARI SILVA THAT YOU MIGHT LIKE 104

YOUR FREE GIFT (ONLY AVAILABLE FOR A LIMITED TIME) 105

REFERENCES 106

Introduction

Paganism is considered by many to be an archaic religion that has no relevance in today's world, but this is far from the truth. Paganism has a lot to teach you, especially its concepts of the world and human life, which differ drastically from other mainstream religions. In this book, you will not only learn about Paganism's history and principles, but you will also get a grounded outlook on Paganism and how it stretches its significance into contemporary life. It would be a mistake to think of Paganism as irrelevant. This is made evident by the number of movements today that look toward ancient Pagan practices for inspiration, such as the global environmental movement, counter-cultural spiritual groups, and even academic scholars.

While most people tend to have a limited outlook on Paganism, considering it to have existed only in ancient Europe, this book stretches beyond such pre-conceptions. In this book, you will be able to learn about Pagan ceremonies and rituals from places all over the world, such as Polynesia, Latin America, Central Asia, and so on. This book is written with a specific eye toward understanding what the term "Pagan" implies, the practices it includes, the communities that fall under it, and how they differ.

Rather than offering a simplistic outlook, this book aims to delve deeper by explaining the fundaments of Paganism while updating the reader on the latest debates surrounding the different facets of Paganism. You will find references to Pagan practices from all over the world, how similar these practices are to each other, the historical background behind them, and even the cross-cultural connections that have led to the evolution of these complex religions and the people who follow them.

Lastly, rather than simply informing you about history, this book will update you on the contours of modern Paganism as well. Many Pagan cultures have gone through years of cultural erasure that have led many to assume that such religions are purely historical concepts. This book challenges such notions by showing how these cultures and their practices continue to survive today because of the revivalist force of the people who have faith in their spiritual inheritance. We will also look at Neo-Pagan cultures that differ considerably from traditional practices, such as atheist and agnostic Pagans who have found a unique way to utilize Pagan principles while rejecting the belief in gods and goddesses.

What emerges at the end is a compelling history of Paganism and the form in which it exists today. With the help of this book, you'll be able to learn about different forms of Paganism, belief systems, cosmologies, myths, practices, rituals, and how you can practice Paganism today. By giving you an array of materials for inspiration, the purpose of this book is to make sure that you can find your own path toward spiritual attunement and rejuvenation.

Chapter 1: Paganism Throughout the Ages

In everyday discourse, Paganism is associated with witchcraft and religious rituals that most people perceive to be ancient and unscientific. The history of Paganism is important because it tells us about the ritualistic practices and belief systems of people in the past, especially Christianity, which led to a widespread dismissal of such ways of thinking about the world. Paganism is a complicated and widespread belief system – the central tenets of Paganism revolve around nature worship and mythologies that animated the world.

It is common in popular culture to perceive Pagans as people who were simply in awe of the world because they did not have a rational scientific understanding. In this book, we will go beyond such simplistic perceptions to help you to study what Paganism was all about, what the common practices of the people were, and how you can learn from them in today's world. This section will focus on what Paganism means, how it has changed throughout history, and what modern Paganism entails.

Paganism, as a term, came into existence only after the development of Christianity. All the ancient belief systems that were pervasive across Europe were lumped together under the term "Pagan." The purpose of this action was to categorize all the ancient European belief systems that came before Christianity as merely barbaric and less developed because of their reverence for simple things such as water and stones. For the Christians, these belief systems represented a problem because they did not conform to the Christian belief of a single God. Different religions existing before Christianity, including Roman and Greek mythologies, were termed "Pagan" and slowly eroded in conversion and various conquests in the name of Christianity.

The term was specifically used for those faiths with a polytheistic system, faiths that believed in more than one God. The class dynamics of those who believed in Paganism are also essential to understand its growth and origins – most Pagan belief systems were rural and were commonly practiced by the provincial peasantry.

The term "Pagan" carried certain negative connotations and was used as a pejorative term for alternative faiths and the country dwellers who believed in them. Pagans were considered less educated, and their faith was dismissed due to their lack of education. The modern Pagan movement has worked hard to change these preconceived notions about Paganism and to establish it as a legitimate religion that deserves respect. The backbone of the modern movement is witchcraft or the "Wicca" movement that continues to believe in medieval practices of witchcraft while pushing the message that witches are not followers of Satan or evil forces as had been publicized in popular culture. Instead, they aim to recognize witchcraft as a legitimate form of belief – one that is essential for their identity, history, and sense of being. Their connection to the world around them is established through witchcraft, which they consider to be a form of power and generational wealth.

Many movements even want to move beyond the title of being merely a religious group and recognize themselves as spiritual groups. One example of this is Druidism. Druids were priests who carried out religious practices of pre-Christian Celtic followers. Their religion is based on a reverence for nature and a denial of any codification since they followed no single sacred text that could be considered the final authority on all matters. Their belief systems are also likely to change based on the interaction and interpretations of new believers who join the system. All these modern movements, including new wave, urban shamanism, etc., are considered Neo-Pagan movements with medieval Paganism as their source and inspiration, yet at the same time having developed key differences that separate them from ancient Paganism.

Paganism has been increasingly popular because of people's disillusionment with popular belief systems that seem too didactic. For many, it is a way of going back to belief systems whose nearness and connection to the world reveals the hidden, vivifying essence of nature. While being a mostly European phenomenon, Paganism has impacted a vast number of religions and is not just limited to the boundaries of Europe. The return of Paganism to parts of Europe occurred in the 19th century, and many disparate groups slowly adopted it as a way of life in the 20th century, leading to the formation of modern and Neo-Pagan movements.

The Meaning of Paganism

Too many scholars, the term "Pagan" is inadequate to describe the diversity and complexity of the pre-Christian belief systems. It is also considered historically inaccurate because, in many ways, it is a term that is in itself a negation. What does that mean? Simply that it's not a positive term, but a negative one – the term Pagan was never used by the people who practiced such a faith but was given to the practice by Christian scholars who needed a term to separate themselves from these supposedly heathen practices.

The term was used to derive a distinct Christian identity – to be Christian meant that you were not Pagan. The term carries on these negative connotations, and it's important to understand the history to make sure you do not fall back on the simplistic views of Paganism as it was used then.

The term Paganism was made popular during the Renaissance by many Christian writers trying to create a new Christian faith different from the supposedly barbaric and heathen practices of the Middle Ages and Classical antiquity. The term is derived from the Latin word "Paganus," which means a "country dweller or a rustic" – this etymology of the term tells us how Paganism and especially the religious conflicts surrounding it were not merely about faith but also land and locality. The fact that a person's religious beliefs were described based on their place of dwelling tells us how the change in living circumstances with the growth of towns and cities suppressed the spiritual practices of those who lived within society's margins. You can see that Paganism was a label used for country folk, thought of as simple.

For most people who followed Pagan belief systems, self-identification mostly took the form of ethnicity, which is why they referred to themselves as simply Romans, Egyptians, Celts, etc. The lumping of multiple belief systems into the umbrella term "Pagan" had many ramifications because it allowed those who created such labels to build an identity of Paganism without getting into specifics. The term became popular because of its convenience, while accuracy and respect of the different forms of Paganism became seemingly less important.

Definitions were one of the most important ways Christianity replaced Paganism because, in many Pagan religions, there wasn't any form of codification or even categorization. For most, the term "religion" itself would have been strange because they did not identify with such a conceptualization of their customs and traditions. They simply considered their rituals as the way of life that had to be passed down from one generation to the other. This allowed much fluidity since the myths kept evolving each time rituals were passed down from one generation to the next. For example, what's considered the "Norse" religion of the Vikings is only a trace of what it once was. Christian authors who heavily edited and censored their customs wrote all the recordings and the texts related to them, biased toward Christian belief.

History

The history of Paganism is spread over multiple eras and geographies, covering many parts of the world. This section will cover how Paganism was formed, how it evolved, its decline, and its resurrection.

Classical Antiquity

For a long time, the Paganism of classical antiquity, especially Greece and Rome, was considered one that did not make a separation between spiritual and political life. In many ways, the customs and mythology that the people believed in came to determine their material everyday existence. The philosopher Ludwig Feuerbach defined Paganism of classical antiquity as "the unity of religion and politics, spirit and nature, of God and man." He saw the Greeks and Romans' beliefs as being tied to their ethnic identity so that the gods they believed in were also tied to their racial individuality. This led to the creation of Pagan traditions that were national religions. In many ways, these belief systems that all people followed connected different concepts such as nature, spirit, national boundaries, and ethnicity through religious customs and traditions.

Many modern historians viewed this relationship between spirituality and politics differently. For them, Pagan movements were cults with a secondary civic application. This conceptualization allows us to understand the interaction between different Pagan groups within the context of the larger society they occupied. Since there was no written code, Pagan belief systems did not automatically fold into nationalistic ideologies but were carefully utilized to create a sense of unified identity. Many dissented and did not believe in the generalized and codified customs sponsored by the state.

Late Antiquity and Christianization

Late Antiquity is considered the time of the expansion and decline of the Roman Empire. This was also when the concept of Paganism came into being since there was a growth of contesting religious belief systems such as Christianity and Judaism that were monotheistic cults. In many ways, Christianity rewrote Pagan belief systems' texts to create its religion that was established as the one true religion at the time, while branding all other belief systems as heathen and having their roots in "false gods." The cult of Dionysus, the god of wine and revelry, was recast in different ways to create the image of Christ as the wandering rabbi, the divine savior whose kindness and joy of life stood in opposition to the evils of the world. It is important to note the strategic use of objects borrowed from Hellenic myths, such as wine and similar iconography, representing Christian ideologies. Such iconoclastic representation challenged Pagan deities while at the same time pushing Christian ideology that held Jesus to be superior to Dionysus.

Pre-Islamic Paganism

Contrary to popular opinion, Paganism was never limited to Europe but was pervasive in the Middle East and the Far East. Arabic Paganism was slowly driven out with the rise of Muhammad and the rapid Islamization of the populous. This process was carried out through multiple military conquests that pushed the different tribes into adopting Islamic codes and abandoning their rituals and temples.

Early Modern Paganism

Paganism was slowly revived by people alienated from Christianity after the Middle Ages and was seen as a revival of indigenous connections to the world. The Renaissance saw an increasing interest in the arts and philosophy of the ancient world as a source of inspiration for the humanist faith essential during this period. Ethics and morality saw a huge contestation as texts from classical antiquity were revived and challenged Christian tenets. During the 16th century, religious hysteria in Britain led to people's mass exodus from blind faith in Christian institutions. With the Reformation, Britain became a Protestant nation rather than a Catholic one. This led to many religious battles, and persecution of dissidents became a common practice. Many people who still connected to their local lands, who still used herbs for medicine and ran local apothecaries, were persecuted as being "witches" – this hysteria was a form of spiritual cleansing against all forms of deviant beliefs. After the 16th and 17th centuries, it became easier for people to access belief systems outside of Christianity as the religious hysteria died down and the study of texts from classical antiquity became the cornerstone of a good education.

Pagan restoration started in the mid-17th century with the revival of Druidism as people became interested in the historical artifacts left by this culture, such as stone formations and healing circles. With the advent of the Enlightenment in Europe, there was an obsession with rationalism and codification that led to mass disillusionment in established and questionable practices. As a form of protest against this, Paganism became increasingly popular in Romantic poetry.

The political applicability of Paganism lay in its animistic and anthropomorphic explanations – instead of seeing the sun as a source of energy, the Greeks, for example, conceived it as being pulled across the sky by the god Apollo. Such explanations vivified the world and made it alive, rather than merely conceiving everything as dead matter as the scientists of the 18th century did. Many Celtic and Viking revivalists saw the nature-worshipping tendencies of these pre-historical tribes as commendable enough to dub them "noble savages." Pagan belief systems were infused into poetry and became the common stock for a new series of legends about nature in romantic poetry. Along with this came new fables and folklore that tried to create a sense of romantic animation tied to creating new nation-states that deployed such Pagan myths to create a perception of a collective self.

The Romantic manifesto was to go looking for the rustic – the common folks' traditions that contained spiritual knowledge passed down from the Pagans. Many centers were opened across Europe to study such traditions as the Far East's spirituality, especially Hinduism and Tibetan Buddhism, and pushed the West into looking at their collective spiritual knowledge. In northern Europe, there was an increasing interest in Norse and Saxon traditions. In Germany, Schelling and Schlegel studied nature religions, and in Eastern Europe, many indigenous languages were revived and the study of ancient runes became common.

Modern Paganism

The interest in witchcraft increased along with these discoveries, and many historians realized that the persecuted followers of witchcraft in the 16th century were underground Pagan cults. It was not until 1951 that witchcraft became a legitimate practice that should not be persecuted. Gerald Brousseau Gardner revealed to the world that he was part of an underground coven of witches practicing witchcraft in secret throughout the ages. The coven he belonged to was known as Wicca, a fertility religion.

Along with this, the counterculture movement in America during the 1960s led to an increased interest in alternative spiritual practices that led to a rediscovery of Native American belief systems and experiments with Taoism and Hinduism. Today, Paganism exists as a belief system for many people who feel its call. Usually, this takes the form of a revival of earlier belief systems, and in the next section, we will discuss the specifics of these beliefs.

Chapter 2: Core Beliefs of Paganism

Paganism consists of multiple philosophies, beliefs, communities, and practices. Together, these systems of thought form a corpus of knowledge that contains ideas of nature, divinity, life, and death. Despite the many differences and multiplicities Paganism contains, there are certain core beliefs of Pagans that will provide direction on what such a religious life would look like.

Nature is central to Paganism. It is the animate and inanimate material world together that is the seat of the divine. The affection, faith, and reverence for the environment make Paganism synonymous with nature. Many gods and goddesses in different pantheons are symbols of nature. The earth becomes the Mother who provides nourishment and sustenance to her children, the inhabitants. The sky is considered the Father, or the overarching deity, which comes together with the earth to make existence possible. The earth, sky, mortals, and deities co-exist in a unity forged by ritualistic practice and care for nature.

Contemporary Pagans are deeply involved in environmental causes and engage in activism to restore the health of the polluted world. Animals are also revered for maintaining the balance of the universe. In present times, the planet has been disturbed by technological and industrial practices. Human beings have become distant from the open forests and rivers of nature. In the old times predating development, the earth was respected for maintaining purity and sustainable living. Such respect for nature resurfaces in Pagan rituals, forging the divine supremacy of nature.

Many Pagans follow traditions, or the "Old Ways", preceding Christianity. These ways are non-Abrahamic, meaning that Paganism is different from Christianity, Judaism, or Islam. Pagans believe in ancestral practices passed on from generation to generation. For example, the cycle of seasonal change has a deeply religious connotation for Pagans. Holidays celebrate the harvest season, the celestial bodies like the Sun and the Moon, and ancient practices pre-dating Christianity.

Indigenous knowledge systems play a huge part in sustaining nature's health, and this forms the core of Pagan rituals. Paganism may consist of diverse practices, but all of these rituals find their basis in nature's divinity.

All Pagan religions have different conceptualizations of gods and goddesses. Some Pagans are polytheistic, with multiple significant deities, while others are monotheistic, meaning they believe in one supreme God's power. Sects could be both polytheistic and monotheistic, with one God who is superior to all others. For example, Hindus have multiple gods, but they can still believe in the one absolute deity Brahma from whom all others emerge. Gods within Paganism are also symbolic of nature, communities, lineages, and so on.

Time plays a major role for Pagans and is considered sacred. For example, old sites like Stonehenge and Newgrange in England and Ireland have an astrologically specific orientation. The architecture of these historic remains signifies particular dates in the year. The doorways of each site are oriented toward the summer and winter solstice, respectively. This sheds light on the specific perception of time within Pagan living and ritualization.

The Pagan phenomenon that originated in the 20th century relies on a range of folk, mythical, and historical sources to create its sacred time. This is often the case for Pagan beliefs; various traditions also celebrate different holy days. Wicca or religious witchcraft, the most commonly observed type of Paganism, is the strongest indication of Paganism's holy period.

The holy period within Wicca is dictated by the movements of the sun and the moon. Lunar cycles occur every twenty-nine to thirty days, while the solar cycle takes place over a year. The primary activities in the celestial cycle include the new moon and the full moon. Wiccan soloists and groups conduct ceremonies on new and full moons, considering these dates as especially favorable for worshiping the goddesses associated with the moon. Since the length of the menstrual period is sometimes similar to that of the lunar cycle, many Wiccans interpret the phases of the moon as being spiritually associated with the "phases" of menstruation. The full moon depicts ovulation, which indicates a season of fertility, imagination, and constructive interaction with the world. The new moon depicts menstruation and is synonymous with relaxation and retirement from earthly affairs for a time of contemplation and regeneration. Wiccan festivities consider such associations communal, with new-moon practices becoming more meditative and full-moon gatherings more joyful or festive.

The solar cycle as practiced by several Wiccan communities includes eight holidays, typically referred to as the "Wheel of the Year." These holidays entail solstices, seasons, equinoxes, and four agricultural festivals with origins in Irish and British myths. The Wheel of the Year has these festivals:

- *Ostara* is the spring equinox
- *Mabon* is the fall equinox
- *Samhain* is celebrated on or around October 31st
- *Imbolc* is celebrated on or around February 1st
- *Beltane* is celebrated on or around May 1st
- *Lughnasadh* is celebrated on or around August 1st
- *Yule* is the winter solstice
- *Litha* is the summer solstice

Many of these holidays have various titles, often derived from Christian and mostly native sources: Samhain is regarded as Hallowe'en, Mabon is Michaelmas, and Imbolc is Candlemas.

Like the moon cycle, the Wheel of the Year is abundant with meaning and myths. Several rituals over the eight holidays create a running story of the creation, rebirth, and ultimate death of the deity who, throughout the year, is engaged with her consort and births a holy child. One more story linked with the Wheel of the Year is an infinite period of confrontation between two imaginary kingdoms – the Oak King and the Holly King – who consistently overcome one another on the solstice; the Oak King reigns in the autumn, and the Holly King emerges triumphant every winter.

The farming festivals are often synonymous with folklore. Samhain simply implies "summer's end", indicating the beginning of winter, and is synonymous with the end of cultivation and the butchering of animals to prepare for the cold season. It has historically been correlated with death and the interaction with deceased ancestors. Imbolc or "In the belly" is the festival that celebrates the arrival of spring and the period when ewes are lactating while carrying spring lambs. The spring festival hits its peak with Beltane or "The fire of Bel," a festival that represents the beginning of the summer and is sequentially opposed to Samhain. Since Samhain is a tradition of the remembrance of death, Beltane is devoted to the commemoration of existence and fertility. After this, the beginning of the harvest is indicated by the Lughnasadh or "Lugh's festival," which signifies the first harvest. People play games and indulge in other rituals on this day.

Such festivals are not widely practiced by all Wiccans, much less by all Pagans. Their influence among several Wiccan and a few other Pagan schools of thought derives from their simplicity and rich mythical and folkloric content connected with the festive seasons. Traditional festivities synonymous with these festivals predate the beginning of Paganism by several centuries and appear to still be observed in certain countries. For instance, the city of Padstow in Cornwall has celebrated May Day festivities every year, which several scholars claim are the remnants of old cultural ceremonies. The festival of Padstow May Day has been re-invented in Berkeley for the past couple of years – an illustration of modern Pagans taking influence from folklore.

Many Pagans accept the belief that the world is mystical. Even the most common aspects of existence are at least theoretically charged with divine force and promise. Paganism honors all space as sacred or divine, although within this system of absolute oneness, specific locations or sites within the natural surroundings are respected as places of unique divine influence and deserving of respect and reverence.

Examples are Angkor Wat, the Serpent Mountain, Newgrange, Macchu Picchu, the Pyramids of Egypt, the Parthenon, and Stonehenge. All around the globe, various places of prehistoric ritual and religious importance survive today as enigmatic, silent testaments of ancient or Pagan spirituality. Paganism also appeals to those venerable temples for guidance in an endless attempt to restore or reinvent polytheistic, monotheistic, or nature-based dedication.

These human-made locations are also susceptible to categorization within a set of meanings. Examples include burial sites, massive observatories, and other locations without specific theological or ritual significance. Ancient locations are also the focus of creative debate when various scholars propose their understanding of the initial or final significance and function of certain sites. These interpretations add to the mystery.

Besides the locations that were specifically formed by human hands, other unique or identifiable sites worldwide have been subject to spiritual dedication, mostly due to distinguishing geographical characteristics. But this was also because of philosophical concepts connected with those sites. For instance, Hawaii, Tor in England, and Glastonbury are instances of impressive religious sites. Less popular sites are centers of local or regional worship, such as the practice of holy worship in Celtic nations.

Such places usually reach the position of being "sacred" in the hearts of worshippers because of cultural relevance, especially in the form of folklore or mythology. Places identified with ancestral gods or goddesses hold a peculiar meaning even among Pagans of the present day. Impressive trees, plentiful springs of water, and other unique aspects of the planet may be infused with significance, either through mythology or local practice, or even founded by contemporary Pagan individuals or groups who felt attracted to finding or establishing divine significance through a connection with a specific aspect of the natural environment.

Pagan rituals often contain abstract or imaginary types of sacredness. These involve mythical conceptions of the other dimension, such as ritually generated holy space like the "World Between the Worlds" of Wiccans. The idea of sacred space is contained within each person's own potential for internal imagination.

Notions of the alternate world take several shapes. Non-material worlds can reside above, beneath, or intertwined with the physical universe. They can occur in several metaphorical places, like above or below water, in fog, or inside the hollow hills or "fairy mounds." The other dimension may be a place of elegance and awe, yet it could also be a land of risk and threat. It may be occupied by deities, heroes, ancestors, ghosts, goblins, pixies, elves, or other beings perceived as strongly related to nature.

Humans may often explore unearthly worlds, but myths are sometimes unclear on how such a quest can occur. When in the other dimension, a human traveler may have a mission or holy duty to fulfill, may be kept in jail, or may become infatuated by a lovely ethereal figure and then face an awful decision between staying with a partner or going back home to the earthly domain.

Perhaps those "other worlds" occur only in human minds, but even so, they may be significant elements inside the spiritual practice of a person or a community. These adventures into the world of mythical fantasy may be perceived as daunting, therapeutic, inspiring, or profoundly revelatory.

Often Pagan communities and people participate in magical rituals as part of their spiritual existence. Such ceremonies can be spiritual where they offer respect to deities through ritual. They can also be thaumaturgic, which is the attempt to transform the world through sorcery. In certain Pagan rituals, conducting a sacred rite includes creating a restricted area or circle where the power of the ceremony begins. This space is understood as possessing a mystical nature that distinguishes it from the remainder of the material realm.

In Wicca, spiritually inscribed ceremonial circles are believed to establish a "world between the worlds," a metaphysical manifestation between the earthly and the metaphysical realms, granting entry to all planes. Unlike other practices of religion where rituals tend to be done in a particular physical venue such as a temple, the circle of magic is simply a compact holy room that can be telepathically generated for every fresh ritual and removed when the practice is over.

The Neo-Paganism movement represents a revival of pre-historic Pagan traditions. In the 1960s, Paganism also sought a friend in the environmental and feminist revolutions. The ideology of Pagans appealed to many environmental activists, who still regarded Earth as holy and acknowledged Mother Earth as the Great Goddess. The character of the witch was picked up by feminists as a model of an autonomous and strong woman. The Great Goddess became an archetype of inner feminine strength and integrity.

The 1960s antiwar Flower Power and Hippie movements brought with them the revival of the term "Pagan". Associated with literary writers such as Ginsberg, Kerouac, and Thoreau, this movement was particularly anti-materialistic. It took inspiration from Pagan religions such as Taoism and Buddhism. The stress on non-institutionalized spiritual practices within Paganism played a major role in its revival during these movements. The return to nature was forged by Eco-Paganism with stress on nature writing and intimacy with non-institutional settings by boycotting war and state violence. This period acted as fertile ground for nature worship as a political tool. For instance, the Hippie movement stressed the importance of personal freedom, sexuality, and psychedelic experiences to establish closeness with the universe. The ethics of Paganism – community, respect for nature, loyalty, and anti-scriptural worship – converged to formulate the resurgence of these primordial beliefs.

Despite inherent differences, Paganism consists of core beliefs: nature worship, the cycle of life and death, faith in deities, and spirituality directed to the otherworld. The freedom to choose the right path is one of the most important aspects of being a Pagan. The choice to experience liberty and immerse yourself in the cosmic abundance of the universe undoes the rules and regulations of the "old ways" of Abrahamic religions. Paganism comes with its own set of ethical practices, no matter which variation of it you are associated with. For instance, Norse Pagans believe in the "Nine Noble Virtues," for they advocate for a life grounded in the preservation of virtue – Courage, Perseverance, Fidelity, Hospitality, Honor, Self-Reliance, Truth, Discipline, and Industriousness. On the flip side, the Wiccan Rede, which acts as a moral code for the disciples, has no specific interpretation.

It is futile to look for a Pagan code of behavior, yet these historical aspects of ritual and worship play a central role in distinguishing Paganism from other practices. Each religion within the fold of Paganism consists of specific ideas of respect, salvation, worship, and transcendence. The objective of the Pagan religion and its wide reach into movements and communities is a testimony to the diversity of its ideological tenets.

Chapter 3: Hellenic and Roman Paganism

The central premise of Hellenistic Paganism is the worship of Olympian deities. It originated in ancient Greece and, throughout the ages, went through complex changes that make it hard to pin down its practices. The Greek religion fell with the destruction of the Greek civilization, as the Roman Emperor Theodosius I outlawed it in the 4th century A.D. The divinities of the ancient Olympian pantheon represented different attributes of the world, forming a sense of being for the people who practiced this religion and believed in its mythologies.

The gods represented nature, the underworld, and heroism; their non-physical form was supposed to represent control over a certain domain of the world. The modern-day Hellenistic polytheists tend to believe in only certain aspects of the culture, but what is essential for them is the belief in the Greek values of moderation, hospitality, and reciprocity.

In this belief system, there is no central law or institution that determines the system's tenets. No hierarchy exists between different priests, and in most cases, the gods can be reached directly by the person praying, without the need for middlemen such as the clergy.

Individual worshipers learn about the rituals and the gods by themselves, doing their own research, which allows for flexibility in beliefs and an inclusive form of representation since the attributes of the gods can be interpreted in a variety of ways.

Although there is no one sacred text or even commandment that determines Hellenistic worship, historical texts are loosely used as references for interpreting different customs and rituals. These include texts from Homer, Hesiod, and other writers of antiquity. The main value that governs the behaviors of those who believe in Hellenistic Paganism is *eusebeia*, also known as piety. It's a restriction imposed on the self that compels one to always continue to believe in the holiness of the deities, no matter what. It's a form of inner maturity that is expected from the followers.

Greek Religion

The twelve Olympian gods led by Zeus were fundamental to the Greek faith in classical times. These were Athena, Apollo, Artemis, Hera, Zeus, Hephaestus, Poseidon, Hades, Hermes, Aphrodite, Ares, and Demeter. Each god was honored with stone temples, sculptures, and sanctuaries (sacrosanct enclosures), which, while devoted to a single deity, also included statues celebrating other deities. The city-states performed many rituals and ceremonies during the year, with a special focus on the principal deity of the city, such as Apollo in Corinth and Athena in Athens. Religious tradition often included worshiping heroes, individuals who were perceived as semi-divine. Such heroes varied from legendary characters in the sagas of Homer to historical individuals such as the creator of a community. At the community level, the landscape was packed with holy sites and monuments. Several sculptures of nymphs were located in and around wells, and visually striking sculptures of Hermes were also found on the sides of the streets.

Magic was a fundamental feature of the Greek faith. The oracles would encourage people to discern the divine will through the rustling of leaves, the form of the fire, smoke on the shrine, birds' movement, sounds of the spring, or in the innards of a creature. People were inculcated into secret sects by religious rituals that historically remained hidden. These sects also had the purpose of spiritual development, and it was considered that these cults' influence even expanded to the underworld.

Following the invasion of Alexander the Great, Greek society expanded extensively and became even more similar to the cultures of Egypt and the Near East. Older studies of Hellenistic faith appeared to view this period as one of theological regression, discerning a rise in cynicism, atheism, agnosticism, mysticism, occultism, and astrology. There is no cause to believe there was a drop in the practice of conventional faith. There is ample historical evidence to show that the Greeks tended to honor the same deities with the same offerings, ceremonies, and festivities as they did in the classical era. New religions also arose in this era, but not to the exclusion of native gods, and only a handful of Greeks were drawn to them.

The defining features of Greco-Hellenism that shared similarities with Paganism were:

Ruler Cults

An interesting phenomenon in the Hellenistic era was the development of cults devoted to the kings of the Hellenistic realms. The first of these was founded under Alexander, whose dominance, wealth, and prestige had raised him to a level that needed unique acknowledgment. His descendants revered him to the extent that, in Egypt, under Ptolemy I Soter, Alexander was revered as a deity.

In doing this, Ptolemy applied older Egyptian concepts of pharaonic worship. Elsewhere, traditions varied. The king could obtain holy recognition without complete classification as a deity, as happened in Athens in 307 A.D. when Demetrius I Poliorcetes and Antigonus I Monophthalmus were honored as saviors (*soteres*) for the salvation of the nation and, as a consequence, a shrine was constructed, a yearly celebration was established, and the position of "priest of the Saviors" was established. Temples devoted to kings were uncommon, but their idols were sometimes installed in other temples, and the rulers would be revered as "temple-sharing gods."

Magic and Astrology

There is considerable evidence that during this era, the use of mysticism and sorcery was common. Oracular temples and sanctuaries were also quite common. There is a lot of documentation regarding spells and charms. Symbols would be put on the homes' gates to receive good luck or dissuade misfortune from falling on the inhabitants inside. Ornaments, often fashioned from valuable or semi-valuable stones, had a defensive ability ascribed them. Figures constructed of copper, gold, or terracotta were drilled with nails or pins and then used to cast magic. Curse tablets made of stone or brass were used to cast curses.

Astrology — the idea that planets and stars affect a person's destiny — was founded in Babylon, where it was initially only applicable to the king or country. In the Hellenistic period, the Greeks developed it into a phenomenally complicated method of Hellenistic astrology. The belief in astrology developed exponentially from the 1st century B.C. onward.

Philosophy

The Hellenistic doctrine provided an alternative to conventional religion. One of these theories was Stoicism, which claimed that existence was to be performed in compliance with the logical structure that the Stoics assumed regulated the universe. Humans had to recognize their destiny as divine will, and moral deeds had to be done following their own inherent significance. Another theory was Epicureanism, which claimed that the world was prone to the atoms' spontaneous motions and that existence should be pursued to achieve internal fulfillment and avoidance of suffering. Other doctrines included Pyrrhonism, which taught that one could achieve inner harmony by a suspension of judgment; Skepticism, which demonstrated disdain for custom and worldly belongings; and Platonism, which adopted the principles of Plato and Peripatetics who upheld Aristotle's teachings. To a certain extent, these ideologies tried to fit into the existing Greek faith, but the thinkers, and those who trained under them, remained a tiny elite community mostly confined to the educated class.

Ceremonies

The absence of a single priestly group implied that there never existed centralized and authoritative religious scriptures or procedures. Just as there was no standardized, traditional holy script for the Greek belief system, there was no uniformity of rituals. Instead, religious activities were coordinated at the community level, with priests typically being drawn from the magistrates of the town or village or receiving jurisdiction from one of the several holy places. Any priestly duties, such as the management of a specific regional festival, could be granted to a particular family through custom. To a great extent, in the absence of "scriptural" holy texts, religious traditions garnered their legitimacy from history.

Greek rites and practices were held primarily at shrines. They were usually dedicated to one or several deities while hosting the idol of only one specific god. Offerings would be deposited at the altar, such as bread, alcohol, and sacred items. Often meat offerings were made; while much of the food was consumed, the leftovers were burned as a sacrifice to the deities. Libations, mostly wine, would be given to the deities, not only in temples but also in their daily life, such as after a colloquium.

One of the rituals was the *pharmakos*, a ceremony involving the removal of a nominal person, such as a slave, from a village or town in a period of distress. It was assumed that by throwing out the Ceremonial Sacrifice, the misery would pass with it.

Sacrifice

Devotion in Greece traditionally included sacrificing household livestock ritually with prayers at the altar. The sacrifice was beyond any temple jurisdiction and was not connected with it at all. The creature sacrificed had to be an ideal specimen of its species. It was adorned with wreaths and guided to the altar in a parade. A child with a basket on his arm would carry a secret blade and lead the procession. After different ceremonies, the creature was executed on the altar. All the females involved wailed out in loud, shrieking tones. The blood was gathered and spread over the altar. Different internal organs, limbs, and other indigestible pieces were burned as the deity's part of the sacrifice, while the meat was extracted to be cooked for the attendees to consume and the leading person sampled it on the spot. The temple generally retained the skin and put it on sale for tanners. The irony that humans had a greater need for sacrifice than the gods never escaped the Greeks, so it became the focus of ridicule in Greek satire.

The Greeks wanted to think that the animal was grateful to be slaughtered, and they regarded different acts of the animals as indicating this. Divination by inspecting sections of the slaughtered body was much less essential than in the Etruscan or Roman religions, but it was performed, particularly with the liver, and especially as a component of the Apollonian sect's agenda. Usually, the Greeks placed more confidence in the study of the actions of birds.

For an easier sacrifice, a drop of incense may have been poured into the holy fire, but this would have been outside of the city, while peasants offered basic sacrifices of a crop harvest as the "first fruits" were picked. *Libation*, a ceremonial draining of liquid, was a component of daily existence. Beverages were used to offer prayers at home; any time wine or a similar alcohol was consumed, a part of the cup's contents was offered as a prayer. More formal libations were used on altars in shrines, and other liquids, such as olive oil and honey, could also be used.

Roman Religion

Roman religion put an overwhelmingly dominant focus on cult activities, filling them with the sacredness of nationalist practice. Roman rituals were compulsively diligent and formal but if the numerous political layers that have accumulated on them through the years can be removed, traces of very early thinking can be easily found. The Greeks had already moved a long way into complex, theoretical, and often adventurous concepts of spirituality. But the organized, dogmatic, and relatively uncouth Romans never gave up their ancient traditions. Before the Greeks' vibrant visual creativity started to affect them, they did not much indulge the later Greeks' passion for imagining their gods in a unique human shape and providing them with their own set mythology.

Pagan Object Worship

A kind of nervous reverence was applied to roles, activities, and artifacts that induced a conviction that was more than ordinary. This sensation was provoked, for example, by streams and forests or by stones that were sometimes considered to be meteorites — that is, they had evidently entered the planet in an unusual way. Adding to this were items of human activity, such as burial sites and frontier stones, and mysterious items, such as Neolithic instruments (often enigmatic meteorites) or bronze helmets (objects that were encountered through the interaction with other cultures).

Divinity in Activity

Early Romans, likes many Italian tribes, perceived human actions as divine. They believed that actions contained a sense of power and force. This is why Romans were obsessed with their functions, since it allowed them to occupy a space of spiritual significance – the acts performed to fulfill a certain activity were considered to be rituals in themselves. All activities were consecrated as sacred, including non-human actions such as the growth of plants or the movement of the sun across the sky. This reverence was extended to everyday activities and certain unique actions were performed only at certain times, like the cry of lament for the death of one's beloved.

Sacrifice and Magic

Divine roles and artifacts appeared to have been invested with energy, since they were enigmatic and disturbing. The early Romans assumed that certain powers had to be worshiped and cajoled to maintain their food sources, physical security, and population increase. Sacrifice was important. The sacrificing substance would reinvigorate the gods – deities were perceived as forces of motion and thus prone to losing energy if they were not reinvigorated. Through this nourishment, they would become competent and willing to satisfy any demands put on them.

Imperial Cult

After the protracted atrocities of the civil war had stopped (circa 30 B.C.), the triumphant Octavian, the adopted child of the tyrant Caesar and creator of the imperial empire, determined that the Pagan faith was far from extinct. His instinctive conviction that the tragedies of the past had been triggered by the giving up of collective religious duties led to the revival of the faith in all its different facets. Octavian also took the title of Augustus, a name that indicated a claim of honor. This did not render him a deity in his lifespan. The many cults dedicated to him prepared the path for his posthumous veneration, just like Caesar. The establishment lionized them both because they appeared to have offered gifts deserving of a god to their nation, Rome. This tradition is identical to the Greek ruler's cult mentioned above.

Chapter 4: Heathenry, Asatru, and Odinism

Asatru emerged before Christianity in northern Europe. The citizens practiced different religions specific to the territory. Among them, Asatru was popular in Scandinavia, Germany, the Netherlands, and England. It is an indigenous faith of the inhabitants of these regions. The term Asatru, from the Norse spoken in ancient Scandinavia, can be translated to "belief in Gods". Norsemen referred to the various practices attached to their faith as Asatru. Asatru were often alluded to as heathens. It is often linked to Wotanism, Germanic Paganism, or Woodanism. Popular books detailing the wisdom of Asatru are the Eddas and the Sagas.

Asatru is a faith that entails worshiping ancient Germanic deities and spirits. It was officially founded in Iceland in the 1970s through the actions of Sveinbjörn Beinteinsson and others who opposed Christianity and conducted *Launblót*, or secret offerings, to the ancient pre-Nordic Pagan gods – a tradition recognized in Iceland because "*Kristnitaka*" was historically deemed the Christianization of Iceland. *Launblót* implies "faith in the *Æsir*"; the *Achatsir* are the Germanic deities.

Asatru is a faith with multiple deities. Many of them, like Thor, have gained significance in popular culture. Asatru was systematically destroyed over hundreds of years, and its non-Christian practices were repressed. The monolithic nature of the Church demonized Pagan practices and led to the eventual downfall of Asatru. Its teachings and ideas lived on through enduring oral histories, traditions, and folklore. The faith has resurfaced in contemporary times through the Neo-Pagan movement in Europe.

Myths and Legends of the Asatru

The condition of the gods and their relationship with many other creatures such as the *jötnar*, who may have been allies, lovers, enemies, or relatives of the deities, are fundamental to the narratives of Norse mythology. As illustrated by reports on names of family and places, Thor was the most famous deity among the Scandinavians throughout the Viking Period, depicted as unceasingly chasing his enemies with Mjölnir, his powerful hammer which could annihilate mountains. In Norse legends, Thor laid waste to several jötnars who were rivals of the deities and mankind. He is married to the glorious deity Sif who is described as having golden hair.

The lord Odin is often listed in the historical documents of the Norse period. He is described as having one eye, a wolf and a raven at his side, and a shield in his hand as he pursues information all over the planet. A legend describes the hanging of Odin on the divine tree of Yggdrasil upside down for nine days in an act of self-sacrifice. His purpose was to acquire an awareness of the runic alphabet that he transmitted to mankind. Odin is depicted as the king of Asgard and the chief of the Aesir. Odin's spouse is a powerful deity, Frigg, who had the power to predict the future but kept it a secret, and they shared a son named Baldr. The child had a set of visions regarding his imminent death. To rid Baldr of his misery, Loki orchestrated his demise. After this, Baldr lived in Hel, a kingdom dominated by a creature named similarly.

Odin was forced to give half of the souls under his command to Freyja, a competitive deity. Descriptions of her were stunning and sensual, as she sported a cape with feathers and performed *seiðr*. She flew to the war to pick between the fallen and took the selected souls to the field of the afterlife, called Fólkvangr. Freyja mourned her lost husband Óðr and looked for him in distant lands. Freyja's sibling, the god Freyr, is often listed in existing texts. His relationship with climate, monarchy, human sexuality, and cultivation provides harmony and joy to mankind. Profoundly in lust, after having caught sight of the lovely *jötunn* Gerðr, he finds her and earns her love, but at the expense of his potential doom. He is fathered by the mighty god Njörðr. Njörðr symbolizes seafaring, abundance, ships, and wealth. He is married to his niece, the mother of Freya and Freyr, known as Skaði. Collectively these gods are called *Vanir*.

Various creatures beyond the deities are described. Dwarves and elves are frequently referenced and tend to be linked to the gods, but their characteristics are unclear, and the bond among them is uncertain. Elves are portrayed as sparkling and lovely, whereas dwarfs mostly behave as smiths of the earth. A community of creatures sometimes defined as trolls, jotnar, and *Thurar* emerge as giants in the folklore. These entities can either participate or hold positions among the gods. *Dísir*, *Norns*, and the Valkyries are often prominently featured in folklore. Although their duties and responsibilities can intersect and vary, they are all feminine entities synonymous with destiny.

Within Norse theology, all things exist in the "Nine Realms" based on the metaphysical tree of Yggdrasil. The deities occupy the celestial world of Asgard, while mankind resides in Midgard, an area in the middle of the universe. Besides deities, humans, and jötnar, these Realms are populated by creatures such as elves and dwarves. Traveling through dimensions is also described in Norse legends, where gods and other creatures may communicate personally with humans. Various animals reside on the island of Yggdrasil, like the rude squirrel Ratatoskr acting as a messenger and the hawk named Veðrfölnir. The tree has three primary branches, and at the bottom of each root there is a trio of feminine deities. Aspects of the world are personified. For instance, the Sun is symbolized by the goddess Sól, the Moon by Máni, and the Planet by the female deity Jörð. Day and nighttime are symbolized by Dagr and Nótt, respectively.

Life after death is a fascinating subject in the folklore of the Asatru. The deceased is exiled to the dark world of Hel — a realm governed by a female being whose valkyries ferry their souls to Odin's hall of marriage, Valhalla. The female deity Rán may appear to those who perish at sea, and the deity Gefjon is reported to have tended virgins after their passing. Texts often refer to reincarnation. Time itself is interpreted as cyclic and linear, and researchers have suggested that circular time was the original mythological conception. Various aspects of the history of cosmological formation are given in Icelandic literature. There are also references to the eventual death and regeneration of the planet — Ragnarok — in folkloric documents.

Heathenry

Heathenry, known as Heathenism, is a modern Pagan faith that draws from pre-Christian traditions. It can be classified as a "new religious movement." Established in Europe at the beginning of the twentieth century, its adherents based it on the value structures of the Germanic Iron Age through to the first half of the Middle Ages. To recreate these former belief structures, Heathenry utilized remaining cultural, historical, and folkloric information as a foundation.

Heathenry is not limited to a specific theology, but it is usually polytheistic, centered on a legion of gods and goddesses from pre-Christian Europe. It takes cosmological beliefs from these previous civilizations and advocates an animistic interpretation of the universe in which the material environment is infused with souls. The supernatural beings are honored in sacrificial rituals called *blóts*, where they are given food and water. These are followed by the ceremonial toast to deities known as *symbel*. Adherents are often engaged in ceremonies intended to cause a trance with metaphysical visions. This practice aims to seek guidance from the gods. Some individuals practice faith on their own. Many Heathens meet in informal clusters, commonly called *hearths* or *kindreds*, to conduct their rituals in either specially-built houses or outdoors. There is an emphasis on integrity, honor, and loyalty within the Heathen code of conduct, but post-life beliefs differ and are seldom highlighted.

The Romanticism of the nineteenth and twentieth century emphasized facets of the pre-Christian cultures of Germanic Europe, which led to the formation of Heathenism. *Völkisch* communities openly worshiping the gods of these cultures appeared in Austria and Germany from 1900 to 1910. They ceased to exist after the downfall of Nazi Germany in the Second World War. The 1970s saw the resurgence of Heathen groups founded in North America and Europe, which were legitimized as organizations. A key divide arose among the Heathens over the topic of race. Older communities often embraced a racist mentality known as "*folkish*" by presenting it as a cultural or racial tradition with intrinsic links to the Aryan-Germanic race. They insisted that white people from northern Europe should be the only practitioners. Such views often caused Heathenry to be associated with white nationalist and far-right viewpoints. Conversely, Heathens embrace a "universalist" viewpoint, arguing that faith is available to all, regardless of ancestry.

Practitioners are trying to restore these past value structures by utilizing ancient background sources. The literary and historical documents included are ancient Norse manuscripts linked to Iceland, like the Poetic and Prose *Edda*, ancient English Literature works such as *Beowulf*, and German texts like *Nibelungenlied*. Heathens often draw from archaeological records on pre-Christian folklore from northern Europe and succeeding periods of history. This content is considered "Lore" among many Heathens and learning it is a significant aspect of their faith. Certain literary documents remain questionable as a way of "reconstructing" pre-Christian belief structures. Since Christians have composed them, they only address pre-Christian faith in a biased and fragmented fashion. Sociologist Jenny Blain defines Heathenry as "a religion constructed from partial material," whereas the theological historian Michael Strmiska explains its practices as "riddled with confusion and historical uncertainty," and thus defining it as something unstructured.

Although the word "Heathenry" is commonly utilized to define religious belief as a whole, many communities prefer distinct classifications shaped by their geographic roots and ideological orientations. Heathens concentrating on Scandinavian traditions sometimes use Ásatrú, *Forn Sed*, or *Vanatrú*. Those focusing on Anglo-Saxon cultures use Theodism or *Fyrnsidu* while those with German cultural practices use Irminism and those who embrace folk and far-right viewpoints strongly favor the terms Wotanism, Odinism and Wodenism, or Odalism. Academic reports state that there are twenty thousand Heathens globally, with groups practicing in Australasia, the Americas, and Europe.

Various Neo-Pagans from German communities commemorate distinct festivals, depending on their religious and cultural orientation, such as Yule, *Sigrblót*, and Winter Nights – all of which have been outlined in *Heimskringla* and have ancient roots. Each festival marks different seasons in northern Europe; the Winter Nights festival marks the beginning of winter, the Yule marks midwinter, and the Sigrblot signifies the advent of summer. Other festivals are also celebrated throughout the year by Heathens. These almost always include days commemorating people who battled to eradicate the dominance of Christianity in Europe or individuals who led troops to new lands. Several Heathen groups have celebrations devoted solely to a particular deity.

A few other Heathens commemorate the eight festivals on the "Wheel of the Year," a culture that Wiccans also follow like other modern Pagan collectives. Others embrace just six of such celebrations, as portrayed by a six-part Wheel of the Year. These contemporary ways of celebrating are criticized by traditional heathens. While festivals can be held annually on pre-decided dates like Christmas, Heathen populations often use the end of the week for celebrations. This makes it possible for working practitioners to participate in the festivities. Throughout these rituals, the Heathens often narrate poems to praise the gods. They usually borrow or mimic early medieval lyrics composed in Norse or English. Alcoholic drinks like ale are consumed and offered to the gods, while torches, candles, and fires are lit. Meetings called "Things" are also held according to territories by the Heathens. These are spiritual ceremonies with workshops, food stalls, festivals, and games. The United States has two national Heathen meetings, called *Trothmoot* and *Althing*.

Ethics and Morality

Heathenry follows core ideas of morality and ethics which can differ across regions and individuals. These are generally drawn from northwestern Europe in medieval times and the Iron Age. The champions of Norse legends are used as inspiration for desirable moral characteristics. A few of the core beliefs are hard work, courage, hospitality, honor, integrity, and loyalty. Being loyal and respectful to family members is considered supremely important. The system of oath-keeping ensures that people keep their promises, as honesty is central to being a Heathen. This leads to an ethos of individual responsibility that focuses on good deeds and fair practices. The concept of sin is widely rejected by Heathens, as they view guilt as destructive rather than constructive. Formal codes of conduct are legitimized in compilations like the Nine Noble Virtues, inspired by ancient texts like the Poetic Edda. These compilations have gathered split responses; some believe they are dangerously dogmatic, while others push for a more concrete assertion of distinct German identity.

There are ethical conflicts within the Heathen community based on conservative assertions. Many members are against the non-conformist and non-traditional actions of their co-religionists. They assert that people must follow the right decorum. The dogmatic members, for instance, refuse to worship Loki due to his relationship with gender-bending. The homophobic populations of Heathens often unfairly criticize LGBT folks, whose rights are under constant threat. Progressive groups celebrate gods like Odin and Thor for their non-conformist gender practices underscored in myths. The Stockholm Pride Parade, for instance, saw the use of Freyr's statue as a symbol of identity assertion.

Politically, Heathens are involved in environmental issues, and many members identify Heathenry as a nature religion. Common ecological activism includes campaigning against ecologically harmful construction, planting trees, protesting against the felling of woodlands, raising funds for saving forests, and so on. Heritage locations are important for many Neo-Pagans, like the German Heathens, who are stressed by the rapid excavation of sacred sites. These locations are linked to ancestral ties, and according to them, it is disrespectful to disturb culturally essential areas.

Thus, from ancient Norse Gods to contemporary Heathens, Paganism has taken many shapes for different communities. The purpose of knowing these myths is to gather appropriate information about origins, developments, and current practices. If you are intrigued by Neo-Paganism or want to practice Heathenry, such information will help you understand the faith's contemporary nature. You might come across Norse gods like Thor, Loki, and Odin in popular cultures like Marvel movies or comic books. Asatru and Heathen myths are not limited to the communities that practice them but have become intertwined with the world's cosmopolitan cultures.

Chapter 5: Celtic Paganism and Druidry

The Druidic movement emerged from the Romanticist theories of the 18th century about the prehistoric druids. While many early medieval authors, notably in Ireland, had vilified the ancient druids as savages that committed human sacrifice and attempted to prevent the advent of Christianity, late medieval writers venerated what they claimed to be the merits of the druids and redefined them as nationalist heroes, especially in Scotland, France, and Germany. It was also around this time that Conrad Celtis started to spread the druids' depiction as bearded, knowledgeable old men in white robes, an interpretation that proved extremely successful in subsequent centuries. The picture of the Iron Age druids as cultural legends would later appear in England during the Early Modern era, with the Anglican Priest William Stukeley of the 17th century declaring himself a "druid" and publishing a series of famous books in which he asserted that prehistoric megaliths, such as Avebury and Stonehenge, were monuments constructed by the druids.

Many who perform Druidry do so with the help of a profound mystical link encountered through the land and its historical evolution. After they first discover Druidry, most people describe this sensation as a kind of "returning home." It's a feeling that allows one to regain their link with the earth, its inhabitants, past, and heritage. This is more than a mere feeling since it is infused with awe, reverence, appreciation, and recognition of time's constant loop. It encourages sacramental dedication, reverence of the holy, and acknowledgment of the gods (male, female, and androgynous) inside the forces of life. This is the cornerstone of the art of Druidry.

The question of whether current Druidry has a direct connection to pre-Roman Britain is still being examined. Traditionally, Druidry was primarily an oral practice, and there are no documents known that were written by pre-Roman forbearers. Theological and philosophical practices have persisted through myths, poetry, and folklore, thanks to the growth of Celtic scholarship in British/Western thought. A good deal was integrated into Christianity when it arrived in Druidic territories, especially in rural communities where Paganism remained side by side with the emerging faith. In the eighteenth century, the re-emergence of Druidry contributed to the scholarly examination of medieval and classical texts, and most of today's popular Druidic culture is focused on the reading of that literature. This examination persists today, and Druids use it as a gateway to their cultural roots. Today, as a faith, Druidry is always expanding its scope. As a consequence, standardizations of customs are decided upon in Druid gatherings where everyone expresses their unique observations, activities, and festivities.

Features of Druidry

Diversity

Many people believe in Druidry because of its heterogeneity. Equality of speech and a direct attachment to the gods are of utmost significance. Relation to the sacred is found through constant practice and not the religious recitation of scriptures, which are simply the perception or view of another. As a polytheistic faith, individuals dedicate themselves to and worship gods that express various facets of life and heritage. For instance, Cerridwen is the goddess of night, the fading moon, and the chalice of capability. Brighid is the goddess of heat, illumination, and proactive movement. The Druids' rites and customs vary depending on which of the two they worship as their main goddess.

The Druids draw guidance from nature. They were influenced by a wide variety of landscapes throughout the British Isles, which is mirrored in the culture of individual and regional communities or "Groves". The deities and spiritual orientation of Druids influenced by their regional North Sea shore are distinct from those of the Druids affected by the rolling hills and forests of the Cotswolds or the wide Devon moors. Similarly, a Druid grove commemorating the midwinter feast in a Kent urban park would look and sound different from a grove in the Highlands of Scotland, where most of the representatives rely on agricultural or rural forms of subsistence. Winter implies something different to different groves, although both simultaneously respect and pursue a connection with nature.

Druids are often influenced by their predecessors. For the Druid, heritage is not a vague term but a collection of people, each having certain strengths and limitations and their own background of achievement and loss. Druidry's heterogeneity is further reflected through the idea that each individual has a distinct lineage of origins and a unique connection with the ancestors. This becomes obvious as we study religious traditions that center on a certain shrine, scenery, legend or poem, talent or profession. A stone might be significant for a certain person because it was an important marker for their ancestors.

Reverence for life, which is an important aspect of Druidry, often offers a spiritual or ethical foundation that is essential for all Druids. Like any other value system, whether theological or secular, this tenet is perceived with only minor disparities of opinion. Integrity, reverence, honesty, and fairness are of prime significance and form the foundation of all Druid activity. This does not distill Druidry, but it adds to it a certain complexity that is embraced and revered by all its adherents. Ironically, plurality is both a divisive and a unifying aspect of Druid culture.

Festivals

Most of the practitioners of contemporary Druidry observe eight main festivities, which can be further split into Solar Festivals and Celtic Fire Festivals, which can also be classified as farming, rural, periodic, or cross-quarter celebrations. Some groves and persons celebrate only the Solar and others only the Fire festivals. Placed throughout the year, these take place every five-to-seven weeks, and generally the Druids conduct ceremonial sacrifices during this period. The goal of the festivities is to achieve two things:

The Druid becomes spiritually alert to the phases of nature, the cycles, the waves of regeneration and death, and the blessings that the deities give during this period.

The Druid aligns their own spirit to the rhythm of nature surrounding them, interacting with the cycles emotionally and mentally instead of pressing against them and inviting tension, despair, fatigue, passivity, and so on.

Aligning with nature's rhythms assures personal well-being, gratitude, motivated imagination, and a thriving society through a devotional engagement with the deities, elders, and guardians of the land.

Druids often conduct ceremonies during different moon cycles, but the most significant period for each particular Druid depends on their own essence. Druids will frequently gather with their groves during the dark or the new moon; others choose the full moon, and some recognize the quarter moons. This activity promotes and supports the Druid's alignment with the phases of the moon, allowing the members to understand its effect on human situations and the surrounding natural environment.

Philosophy

The purpose of a Druid's activity is to learn to comprehend and establish a holy connection with nature and thus with the deities. Belief means blind confidence, and that's not the Druid approach. Perception and awareness of the spiritual relation are the building stones of the culture, not the dependency on blind confidence in anything that one has not encountered or experienced on a personal level. Most Druids aim to communicate with a common source – nature – and this essence offers several universal bases of knowledge, if not faith. The following items are known as declarations of popular druid learnings.

1. Nature is perceived as sacred no matter what because it's the only way to discern the holy world of experiences created by the gods.

2. An understanding of the more-than-human constantly begets perception of the world as a series of interconnected webs where our actions are linked to each other and have an effect on everything else.

While all are intertwined, this link is not experienced by many people. They stand away from the natural world and, often, expel all extended things out of their own conception of themselves to convince themselves of their superiority to nature. A Druid must use their perceptions and learn to grow them to expand their mind to the true essence that floats around them. This allows one to communicate with the stream of energy that is the spiritual center. In other terms, knowledge of the system is important for a dignified existence. All Druids worship the forces of nature (the Three Realms of Earth,

Water. and Air), heritage (of race, past, and folklore), and knowledge. In terms of a unified faith and practice, Druids are supposed to:

1. Treat the non-human world with reverence, preserve and safeguard nature, and connect with its different rhythms, like the rustling of leaves and the birds' flight.

2. Treat nature constructed by humans with reverence to develop their thinking and internal feelings in a way that leads to mutual empathy for all living beings.

3. To learn about the past and its various contours so that the tradition never dies out. To revive stories through their constant retellings.

All these are sacred activities done not merely to obey the gods, the elders, or the society, but to communicate with the deities, finding a spiritually significant and often joyful unity. Since the deities are powers of nature and ancestry, they appear in every part of the cosmos. Instead of a single symbolic idea of a special imaginative and mystical god, Druids find the sacred with the help of research, ceremony, poetry, reflection, worship, and dance. Through chanting an old tune, studying an ancient tongue, resting at the forefathers' grave or in an ancient stone ring, sitting quietly in the rain, growing vegetables, or cultivating the field, the Druid unlocks his spirit (psyche, ego, soul) to communicate with the powers of nature (deities) existing in that part of the world. They expand their minds to their roots and to the deities who led them toward holy bonds, happiness, and harmony.

Gods and Goddesses

Ana or Danu/Dana – The Primordial Goddess of Nature

Counted as the earliest Celtic deity in Ireland, Ana (also identified as Anu, Annan, Dana, and Danu) likely represented the primeval element of femininity, with her qualities defining her as a maternal goddess. The Celtic goddess, sometimes depicted as a fair and wise woman, was synonymous with nature and the divine spirit while also reflecting the conflicting (yet transient) facets of wealth, intelligence, mortality, and rebirth.

Dagda – The Cheerful Chief of Gods

The most powerful god within the pantheon of the Celtic gods of Ireland, the Dagda 'Strong God' was an all-powerful father figure. Admired as chief of the *Tuatha Dé Danann* clan of deities, he was typically identified with prosperity, cultivation, climate, and patriarchal power, though often exhibiting elements of sorcery, intelligence, science, and animism. These aspects illustrate his popularity and deification by Celtic druids. Many of these features often bear a remarkable resemblance to the supernatural attributes of Odin, the patriarch of the Aesir tribe of the ancient Norse deities.

Aengus (Angus) /Aonghus – The Youthful God of Love

The child of the Dagda and the river-goddess Bionn, Aengus (or Aonghus), meaning "real vigor," was the Celtic god of affection, vitality, and literary imagination. In the legendary story, to conceal his secret liaison and the resulting pregnancy of Bionn, the Dagda (who was the king of the Celtic deities and could mysteriously regulate the climate) held the sun fixed for nine months, which culminated in the birth of Aengus in only one day. Aengus proved to be a vibrant hero with a friendly (if rather quirky) personality who had four birds circling his ears all the time.

Lugus / Lugh – The Courageous Warrior God

Though seldom discussed in the manuscripts, Lugos or Lugus (as identified in Gaul) or his corollaries *Lleu Llaw Gyffes* (Lleu of the Skillful Hand) in Welsh and *Lugh Lámhfhada* (Lugh of the Long Arm) in Gaelic Irish, was a significant god among Celtic divinities. Sometimes worshipped as the shining sun deity, Lugus or Lugh was often portrayed as a suave (and sometimes vibrant) fighter famous for destroying Balor, the one-eyed leader of the *Formorii*, the ancient enemies of the Tuatha Dé Danann.

Mórrígan – The Mysterious Goddess of Fate

Mórrígan or Morrigan (also identified as Morrígu) was regarded as a mystical and somewhat sinister female goddess among Ireland's Celtic divinities, synonymous with both battle and destiny. In modern Irish, the name Mór-Ríoghain is loosely interpreted as the "phantom goddess." In keeping with this enigmatic descriptor, in the legendary story Morrigan was adept at transforming her form (generally evolving into a crow – the *badb*) and foreshadowing destruction, though at the same time stirring men to battle. In contrast to these apparently unpredictable and "battle-minded" qualities, Morrigan was often deified as a Celtic deity of authority who served as the spiritual protector of the earth and its inhabitants.

Brigid – The 'Triple' Goddess of Healing

In comparison to the moping elements of Morrigan, Brigid, in pre-Christianity Ireland, was known as the Celtic deity of regeneration, spring festivals, and craft. In the legendary story, she was the child of the Dagda and thus a part of the Tuatha Dé Danann. Some say that there were various domesticated creatures, ranging from oxen to dogs, that used to call out to the deity in case of a threat.

Modern Druidry

Neo-Druidry has been popularized due to the activities of organizations like The Order of Bards, Ovates, and Druids, which considers Druidry to be a mystical path and activity that appeals to three of our deepest longings:

    To be truly imaginative throughout our existence

    To connect profoundly with the realm of nature

    To seek entrance to a well of sublime knowledge

These longings emerge from different fragments of ourselves that can be embodied as the Shaman, the Sage, and the Singer. In Druidry, bardic principles seek to cultivate the poet, writer, or orator within us, the artistic self; prophetic teachings seek to encourage the shaman, the admirer of nature, the protector within us; Druidic principles seek to grow our knowledge and wisdom, the sage who resides within every one of us.

Druidry, or Druidism, today demonstrates itself in three typically distinct ways: as a linguistic activity to promote Cornish, Welsh, and Breton dialects, as a brotherly endeavor of shared cooperation and fundraising for worthy causes, and as a mystical journey. Each of these various methods relies on the spirit of the early Druids, who were the stewards of the mystical and theological culture that prevailed before the arrival of Christianity and whose presence can be mapped from Ireland's coastline to the west of France – and maybe even further.

Chapter 6: Hinduism and Multi-God Faiths of the Far East

The West generally views the various faiths of the Far East as different types of Paganism. This chapter will explore the Hindu pantheon and Chinese and Japanese mythology to shed light on the polytheistic practices of the Far East. Each god within these traditions represents the divine within the universe. Through iconography, scriptures, and legends, you can understand the diverse nature of these religions.

The most ancient religion on the planet is Hinduism, and it is famous for its complex pantheon of gods. Many historians note that its origins and traditions can be traced back to almost four thousand years ago. In present times, it remains a popular religion with over nine million believers, making it the third-largest faith on Earth. India houses the majority of the Hindu population, as ninety-five percent of them live there. No person is associated with the foundation of this religion, and its historical origin remains uncertain. Diversity is a major feature of Hinduism as it consists of multiple conventions, philosophies, and practices. It is not a single faith organized around fixed practices. It is referred to as a lifestyle or "a way of living" by many. Its rituals can differ across families, communities, tribes, and regions. Hinduism and its forms are sometimes "henotheistic" or organized around the worship of "Brahma," who is considered the most supreme God. Such forms acknowledge the existence of other deities too, but Brahma represents the absolute god. Followers believe there are various paths to unite with the supreme God through diverse ways of worship. One of the Hindu doctrine's basic tenets is *samsara*, or the cycle of birth and death, continuing through reincarnation. This cycle is upheld by the universal logic of Karma or the "law of cause and effect." Karma is the power of an individual's actions, which determines their destiny. Each deed or action exerts a force that impacts the person's life in pleasant or unpleasant ways. For example, if a man commits a crime, his life will be shaped by the bad karma of his negative deed. The law of karma justifies present life conditions as well as the cycle of birth and re-birth. Reincarnation occurs based on the cumulative deeds of an individual, and each person's place in the world is pre-defined by their past actions in previous lives.

Hinduism upholds such beliefs through faith in the soul of living beings or *aatman*. According to this philosophy, each animate thing consists of a soul born out of God's soul. Through good karma and worship, the followers can achieve salvation, or *moksha*, which ends the cycle of re-birth. By being honest devotees, believers want to achieve moksha to become reunited with God's supreme or "absolute" soul.

The central principle of Hinduism is the determination of life through karma. To eliminate negative karma, Hindus aim to follow codes of morality and fair conduct called *dharma*. Examples include respecting traditions, following marriage rituals, doing honest work, and showing kindness to others. Hindus respect each living thing in the world, and animals are symbolic of the divine. The cow is considered sacred and cannot be harmed. Food is ritually essential for the Hindus. For example, beef cannot be consumed as it is disrespectful to the cow. Other dietary restrictions include pork consumption and other non-vegetarian foods. Many Hindus practice vegetarianism as a part of their dharma.

The three central gods of the Hindu trinity are Shiva, Vishnu, and Brahma. Shiva and Vishnu are viewed as supreme in modern times, as is evident in the lack of places of worship for Brahma. Note that "Brahman" and "Brahma" are not the same – the latter is an aspect of the absolute deity Brahman. Yet all gods play a significant role in formulating Hinduism's diversity and represent different schools of thought and groups of believers.

Let us start with Shiva, who is a major deity for Hindus. The name roughly translates to mean "the auspicious one." People who believe in Shiva's supremacy call themselves "Shaivaites." As a Pagan god, he is connected to nature and is known as Pasupati, or "Lord of Beasts." Shiva is not only the creator but also the destroyer. His role as healer, annihilator, ascetic, raging avenger, and kind herder of souls underscores the multiplicity of Hinduism. A popular myth within Hinduism tells how Shiva rescued human existence by swallowing the poisonous waters of destruction in his throat. His famous image with a blue complexion represents this myth.

Specific symbols and iconography exist for Hindu deities through the *Murti*, an image of a god with sentimental and divine value. For Shiva, it is the *linga,* or phallus, and the bull. Popular photos of Shiva represent him as an ascetic with matted hair piled atop his head. The background is of the half-moon and the holy river Ganga. Mythology attributes the rescue of Ganga from destruction by letting her pass through his hair. He is also the great dancer "Nataraja," whose exotic rhythm is considered divine. The diversity of his paradoxical traits are present in the dance of Nataraja. The tension between eternity and finite time is metaphorical of chaos and calm coexisting. As the eternal dancer, he is supreme and divine, yet time represents the limits on human life. Such a paradox is evident in his association with the third eye. He thus possessed both inner sight and the ability to destroy all that is outside. His pictures show him with four hands clasping sacred objects – a hand drum, deerskin, skull, and trident.

Goddesses, or *Devis*, associated with Shiva are Durga, Uma, Parvati, Kali, Sati, and Shakti. In Hindu mythology, Devi is the supreme female deity who represents the mother. The act of giving birth is divine and represents creation. Like the child who witnesses his mother's face first, the Devi is the goddess of maternal power. Mythology attributes qualities of mercy, care, kindness, rejuvenation, and love to the mother deity. The open hand is a symbol of Devi's blessing that heals. Traditions link Devi's existence with the beast Mahishasura, who had a buffalo's face and was an almost undefeatable evil. The creation of the Devi was meant to fix the limited capacity of the gods. Only she could defeat Mahishasura by combining the weapons and powers of each god. The Devi came to represent the totality of the Divine. Another myth places the birth of Devi before Shiva, Vishnu, and Brahma. According to this legend, she not only defeated evil but used her divine virtue and supremacy to unravel the mystery of cosmic existence. As simultaneously a mother and protector, she is symbolized by many arms. Each arm holds different powers needed for the destruction of evil. The female form differs from the uninterrupted egotism and cruel male energy of Mahishasura. Gods within Hinduism do not uphold strict genders. For instance, both Shiva and Vishnu have female forms. Shiva is also called "Ardhnarishwar," which means a god whose other part is a woman.

Another popular Hindu God is Ganesha, the elephant-headed son of Shiva and Parvati. Like the child, he represents friendliness, humility, and approachability. There are many legends about the birth of Ganesha. One of the widely known stories about his birth is his creation at the hands of his mother, Parvati. When Shiva refused to provide Parvati with a child, she created a baby with earthly materials. When he was given the duty to guard his mother's privacy during her bath, he was beheaded by his father Shiva when he suddenly returned home. Struck with grief and anger, Parvati became inconsolable. Shiva then promised to breathe life back into the child by replacing his head with that of the first being he encountered. When an elephant appeared, Shiva replaced Ganesha's head with that of the creature. Many legends also attribute Ganesha's creation to the voluntary sacrifice of an elephant. There is yet another tale about his birth: the burning of Ganesha's head by Sani or Saturn. Proud of her creation, Parvati paraded her child in front of the gods, and when she insisted Sani look at Ganesha, he burnt his head to ashes. His head was then restored by Vishnu's mercy, which saved his life. Myths also credit Shiva directly for creating Ganesha. The Purana tells the tale of his creation as being initiated by the laugh of lord Shiva. Worried that his son was too powerful, he bestowed him with an elephant's head and a hanging belly.

Each legend tells a different tale of the birth and significance of the many gods. The origin stories differ from territory to territory, yet the diversity connects everything together. Within Hindu Paganism, every god is an aspect of the absolute deity. Brahma is the creator, Vishnu is the preserver, and Shiva, as you have read, is the destroyer and the guardian of the universe. All these gods have children, wives, siblings, enemies, and so on. The pantheon is deeply ingrained in nature, morality, and scriptural worship as well. Learning about these legends, stories, and rituals will help you imagine the vivid cultural history of Pagan religions.

Chinese Mythology

Chinese mythology differs from Hindu mythology in many ways. The oral tradition of storytelling within the territory of China makes up the literature of Chinese mythology. It also has variations across groups and territories, and thus it is not monolithic in any way. Several important mythological traditions include the *Han* Chinese and *Huaxia*. Japanese and Tibetan legends are also included. The works written in Chinese are what reveal the central concerns of Chinese myths.

Most Chinese legends consist of adrenaline-heavy stories about supernatural beings and fantastic individuals. These mythologies have been produced through their contact with other religions like Buddhism, Confucianism, and Taoism. Theorists have found a lot of evidence proving that elements of these religions have been integrated within the Chinese mythological tradition. For instance, the dwelling place of gods and immortals in the "Paradise of the Spirit" in Taoism appears in Chinese myths as well.

The shamanic view of the world has come to dominate a wide arena of mythological beliefs. Examples of shamanism include Hmong shamanism of the Miao and Qing Dynasty, and Mongol shamanism. Here too, ritual plays an important role in the sustenance of myths. In parts of China, people burn banknotes or "hell money" as a celebration along with fireworks, festivities, and so on. Yu's legend and the ritual significance of his steps, or *Yubu*, is an example of mythology and ritual intersecting. Yu, the Chinese emperor, is credited with saving people from the Great Flood. The legend says that in saving the people, he developed a limp from extreme fatigue. Daoists have choreographed a similar motion into various locomotive rituals. Practice and mythology merge - Yu's divine sacrifice in the past comes to be related to the present through ritual.

Like Hinduism, Chinese mythology consists of important notions of gender and sexuality. Some myths like that of the mother goddess representing procreation and fertility hint at what scholars such as Jordan Paper call the "patriarchal influence over time." Tu'er Shen, which translates to "rabbit deity," is a homosexual god who reigns over attraction, sex, and love between men. The Chinese language itself consists of a different grammar for gender as compared to English. There are no nouns or pronouns which mark gender in Chinese. Yet, the existence of balance through gender is present within its mythology. The duality of yin and yang is an example of this. Depicted by half black and half white, it symbolizes the coexistence of darkness and light, negativity and positivity, good and evil, etc. The

Chinese creation myth attributes the birth of the world to the organization of chaos into a balanced universe. Ying and yang represent cycles of life emerging out of duality like winter and summer, woman and man, chaos and organization. Within Chinese cosmology, yin and yang represent the divergent material forces of the universe.

Chinese cosmology consists of mythological ideas about man, nature, and the universe. Some legends focus on earth and its nature - especially its relationship to the rest of the universe. A famous understanding of the earth is as a square divided into two by a spherical sky above it. "Sky pillars" or trees, mountains, and other natural phenomena are significant for this division. Heaven is conceptualized as above the earth or existing in the sky with structures similar to those of human societies. An underworld exists below the mortal realm called the *Diyu* or Yellow Springs. It is believed that souls repent for their sins after death in the Diyu by similar bureaucratic laws that exist in heaven and earth. China was seen as the "Middle Kingdom" or the earthly realm.

Japanese Mythology

Japanese mythology offers an interesting look into the relationship between territory and religion. The folktales, legends, and belief systems of Japan emerged out of Buddhist and Shinto mythologies. Japan's proximity to China, Ainu, Korea, and Okinawa legends is essential to its mythological tradition. The Japanese pantheon is diverse, with almost eight million gods and goddesses who are named Kami. There are three original gods who are succeeded by the Kami. The Kami's birth was before humanity, and they are said to have been birthed by the ancient oil of the universe.

Nature is significant for understanding the Kami as they represent natural phenomena. They can take the shape of humans and nature all at once. Many scholars have found that historical records of Kami representation are both human and a hybrid between human and non-human phenomenon. For example, Amaterasu and Ningi of the pantheon are mostly represented as humans.

The Shinto belief system is central to such mythology and still exists in modern Japan. Shinto means spirit and the belief that each part of nature has a Kami. Each deity is symbolized by a myth that explains its purpose and origin, such as mountain gods, river nymphs, and spirits of the wind and seasons. Interaction with religions like Buddhism and Christianity has impacted the Japanese pantheon heavily. Christianity penetrated Japan in the fourteenth century through westerners like St. Francis Xavier.

The Sun and the Moon play a major role in the creation of the Japanese pantheon. Amaterasu, like the kami of the sun, is one of the most important deities. She is one of the "Three Precious Children" along with the Shinto moon goddess Tsukuyomi and storm deity Susanoo. They are born out of the creator, Izanagi, one of the primordial gods.

Chapter 7: Egyptian and Middle Eastern Paganism

The framework of belief and the fundamental structure of Egyptian culture are its founding myths. All dimensions of existence in ancient Egypt were determined by the myths about the construction of the universe and the preservation of the earth by the deities. Egyptian religion affected other societies via trade dissemination and became increasingly popular after 150 B.C. as the Silk Road was established and the Egyptian coastal city of Alexandria became a significant trading hub. The importance of Egyptian myths to other civilizations lies in the propagation of the idea of everlasting existence after death, protective spirits, and rebirth. Roman spiritual traditions were inspired heavily by Egyptian rites, and in Hellenic times, both Plato and Pythagoras were inspired by the Egyptian concept of rebirth.

Human life was recognized by the Egyptians as just a tiny part of the everlasting voyage, ruled over and directed by the divine powers in the shape of the multiple gods that made up the Egyptian pantheon. Historian Matthew Bunson noted how Heh (called "Huh" in some eras) was one of the original gods of Ogdoad, the eight "first" deities worshiped during the Old Kingdom, 2575-2134 B.C., at Hermopolis. In Egyptian religious beliefs, the goals and destiny of all human life were summed up as a stage of existence in which mortals could attain everlasting bliss. One's mortal existence was not merely a precursor to something better but a component of the overall path. The Egyptian idea of life after death was supposed to be an exact reflection of one's existence on Earth. A follower had to conduct his life properly if he planned to happily experience the remainder of his everlasting quest.

Creation Myth

For the Egyptians, the story begins with the formation of the universe out of chaos and turmoil. Once upon a time, there was hardly anything, just limitless darkness lacking shape or meaning. Living inside this vacuum was Heka (the deity of miracles), who waited for the first instance of life. From this muddy darkness, *Nu*, grew the primeval peak, identified as the *ben-ben*, on which resided the supreme deity Atum. Atum gazed at the emptiness and realized his isolation, and then, through the force of sorcery, he coupled with his own reflection to deliver two twins, Shu (the deity of the air, whom Atum spat out) and Tefnut (goddess of moisture, vomited out by Atum). Shu brought the concept of life to the young universe, while Tefnut added the rules of harmony.

Abandoning their parent on the ben-ben, they headed out to create the Earth. In time, Atum grew worried that his offspring had gone too far, so he detached his eye and dispatched it in pursuit of them. After his eye left, Atum stood isolated on the slope in confusion, contemplating infinity. Tefnut and Shu arrived with Atum's separated eye (in later mythologies identified as the eyes of Udjat, or the eyes of Ra) and Atum, thankful for their comfortable arrival, poured tears of gratitude. These tears, falling into the fruitful land of the ben-ben, yielded life to women and men.

These nascent beings had nowhere to dwell, and so Tefnut and Shu copulated and yielded *Nut* (the sky) and *Geb* (the earth). Nut and Geb, though siblings, fell profoundly in love and became indivisible. Atum considered their actions intolerable and forced Geb away from

Nut, far up into the sky. The two were always able to view each other but were not allowed to hold each other anymore. Nut was still pregnant with Geb's children and ultimately gave life to Horus, Nephthys, Isis, Set, and Osiris - the main deities of Egypt who are frequently remembered as the eldest. Osiris proved himself to be a just and fair deity, so Atum granted him the governance of the universe.

Osiris effectively handled the universe, governing with his wife-sister Isis, and determined where the plants would ideally flourish, and the rivers would run more softly. In harmony, he built the nation of Egypt with the Nile River catering to the inhabitants.

In all aspects, he behaved in line with the concept of *ma'at* (balance) and honored his father and his family by holding all matters in a healthy coexistence. But his sibling Set grew jealous of life and also of the strength and beauty of Osiris. He had his brother's precise dimensions recorded in secrecy and then commissioned an ornate box to be made exactly fitting those measurements. When the box was finished, Set held a large feast at which he hosted Osiris and sixty others. At the conclusion of the gathering, he presented the large box as a present to the one who would perfectly fit inside. Osiris, of course, aligned with it and, as soon as he was within the box, Set closed the cover firmly and plunged it into the Nile River. Then he informed all that Osiris was deceased and claimed the governance of the universe.

Isis declined to accept that her spouse was deceased and preceded in pursuit of him, eventually discovering the box inside the tree of Byblos. She took the remains home to Egypt and set out to collect medicines to produce remedies that would lead Osiris back from the dead. When she had concealed Osiris, she contacted Nephthys, her sister, and asked her to protect the place.

Around this time, Set started to fear the discovery of the body of Osiris by Isis. He was concerned that she would devise a means to awaken his consciousness with her formidable strength and experience in matters of life and death. Upon seeing her missing, he questioned Nephthys about her whereabouts, and when the deity responded, he realized she was misleading him. He managed to obtain from her the whereabouts of the corpse of Osiris and went there, ripping the chest apart and breaking the corpse into forty-two parts. To ensure that it would be impossible for Isis to find these pieces, he hurled them across the entirety of Egypt.

When Isis arrived and saw the casket broken and the corpse missing, she collapsed wailing in sorrow. Nephthys, feeling bad for betraying her, informed Isis of what had occurred and aided her in locating the pieces of Osiris. Anywhere a body piece was discovered, they would hide it in the ground and create a temple there to shield it from Set. Thus, the two goddesses founded the forty-two regions of Egypt.

They eventually placed together all the body parts except the phallus that a shark had just swallowed. Isis then produced a substitute piece for the penis, procreated with her spouse, and became pregnant with Horus. Isis ultimately resurrected Osiris, but since he was unfinished, he could not govern the universe as he previously did. Instead, he went down to the afterlife to be the virtuous ruler and lord of the underworld.

Gods & Goddesses

The bodily shape of the numerous Egyptian deities was typically a mixture of animal and man, and several were identified with one or more animal types. An animal would convey the attitude of a god. If a deity were furious, he could be represented as a fearsome lion or, if friendly, a dog. The tradition was to represent the animal deities with humanoid bodies and the face of an animal.

Nut

The parent of Seth, Isis, Osiris, and Nephthys, Nut is typically seen in human shape; her stretched form represents the sky. Each arm reflects a specific position as the form extends around the globe. Nut consumed the sinking sun (Ra) every night and yielded birth to it every day. She is also portrayed on the temples' walls, on the caskets' interior, and the on roofs of the shrines.

Shu

Shu was Tefnut's spouse and Geb and Nut's father. He and his wife were the first deities to be formed by Atum. Shu was the deity of wind and sunshine, or, more specifically, of dry wind, and his wife embodied precipitation. Normally, he was represented as a man donning a headscarf in the shape of a feather.

Shu's role was to carry the body of the deity Nun to distinguish the sky from the land. He was not a sun god, but his involvement in producing sunshine associated him with Ra.

Anubis

Anubis is seen as either a jackal or a jackal-headed man. Osiris was his father and Nephthys his mother. His place of worship was Cynopolis, today recognized as El Kes. He was strongly identified with cremation and as the guardian of the deceased. Anubis took the dead to the judgment chamber.

Khnum

Khnum is the water god of the Nile, also known as the creator of men. He is one of the most ancient deities of Egypt and represents the river Nile itself. It was the job of Khnum to control the floods; he was the guardian of the gate and the one who brought the river forward or held it in check at the right times. He is represented as a ram-headed man with water flowing out of his hands and a potter's wheel by his side.

The name Khnum means "to create", and he is known as the creator of men. He used mud from the Nile to mold people on his potter's wheel while the light of the sun god Ra shone upon him. Then he placed these children in the mothers' wombs.

Hathor

Hathor was Ra's child and the deity of women, marriage, elegance, joy, and art. She is portrayed in three facets: like a cow, as a girl with cow ears, and as a lady sporting a headscarf made of a cow's horn. She carries the solar disk behind her horns in this third embodiment. She was the mistress of Horus, and her name simply meant "House of Horus." She had several prominent shrines in Dendara.

Heh

Heh is a god without any form and represents eternity and infinity, making him the god of long life and time. Heh has no gender since he is endless but can be represented as male or female. Heh is the male aspect, while Hauhet is the female aspect.

Heh is depicted as a crouching man with a frog's head or sometimes as a frog itself with a tadpole in his hand. The female form of Heh is depicted with the head of a snake or as a snake itself. The hieroglyph for one million is an image of Heh holding up his hands; this was considered as infinity during earlier times, and so Heh is also known as "the god of a million years."

Horus

Horus was the child of Isis and Osiris and the foe of the evil deity Seth. He's represented as a hawk or a person with a hawk's head. He is also displayed as an adolescent with hair to one side, lying on his mother's lap. He was the lord of heaven and the divine guardian of the rulers.

Ma'at

Ma'at was the deity of fairness and righteousness, representing the fundamental balance of the cosmos. She was presented as a sitting woman carrying an owl feather. Her influence controlled the weather and the motions of the planets. Ma'at was the guardian of truth and the icon of classical Egyptian morality. Thus, the Cleric, who was in control of the Courts, was designated the Priest of Ma'at.

Nephthys

Nephthys was a protective goddess of the dead. She was the daughter of Geb (god of the earth) and Nut (goddess of the sky). She was a sibling of Isis and Osiris, the sister-wife of Set and the mother of Anubis. In Egyptian mythology, Nephthys means "Mistress of the house," which is why she was the head of the household of gods and women's protector in every household. She is personified as a woman with a long satin dress, carrying a small basket on top of her head with hieroglyphs written on it. She is associated with many things due to her connection to both life and death, such as a crow, a falcon, a hawk, and a kite. Her pictures can also be seen on funeral caskets, as she accompanied the dead in their afterlife, which is why she was also known as the "Friend of the Dead."

Nephthys was married to Set (the god of deserts) but never bore him a child; she did have a child with Osiris, called Anubis. She gave her son Anubis to her sister Isis to protect him from Set. She had a strange relationship with her husband, Set, whom she married but never trusted. When Set learned that Nephthys had a son with Osiris, he set out to kill him, but she stood in his way and tried to stop him. She was close to her sister Isis; they are depicted together in the scriptures as opposite forces, life and death.

Nephthys was a close friend of the dead, and she helped them go into the afterlife and comforted the relatives of the dead at the time of mourning. She is depicted in coffins, caskets, and sarcophagus to protect the contents of the dead. She was a morbid but necessary force that protected and helped the dead. She played many roles –

she was the protector of Hapi, one of the four sons of Horus, who protected the lungs of the deceased. She was also the protector of the Pharaoh in life or death. She could see beyond ordinary sight, and she protected the Pharaoh by incinerating anyone who planned against them. She also passed on this gift to every Pharaoh to look over all of Egypt and protect it.

She is worshiped all over Egypt by nursing mothers because she is a goddess of protection who nursed Horus and the Pharaoh. Her worship was mostly centered within the cities of Heliopolis and Abydos. Major temples dedicated to her are situated at Lunu, Disopolites, Hebet, Per-mert, Re-neferet, Het-sekhem, and Senu.

Thoth

Thoth was the deity of language and intelligence. He was represented as a human with an ibis face, bearing the pencil and the slate of a scholar. The Greeks connected him with Hermes and credited to him the development of all disciplines and the discovery of printing. He is often depicted composing or doing sums.

Chapter 8: Slavic Paganism

You may have heard of vampires, demons, and strigoi in TV shows, books, and literature. While the creatures of Slavic Paganism have become recognizable parts of popular culture, the faith itself is not widely known. It is alleged that the Slavic people invented human sacrifices. This religion has many interesting aspects - horse divination, cosmology, multi-headed idols, and so on. Many Slavic myths about deities like Veles, Triglav, Perun, and Svantevit have become lost as the ancestors did not leave traces of their rituals, practices, and myths. There are few existing records of Slavic myths and prayers, and only some iconography and artifacts exist. Most records have been written by Christian chroniclers who wrote while the Slavic faith was declining.

Records have been reconstructed by scholars who have tapped into ethnology, comparative religion, linguistics, Indo-European studies, archeology, and relics of legends, customs, and Slavic tales.

Slavic Creation Myth

There are three major versions of the Slavic Creation myth. The earth-diver myth is represented by the oceanic symbol and contends that water pre-existed and the earth was born from it, and that God and the Devil coexisted and cooperated for the birthing of the earth. The next version is concerned with the Cosmic Egg (symbol for the beginning) and the World Tree (divine tree supporting the heavens). The final myth argues that the universe was created by dismembering an ancient being.

The first Slavic myth described the beginning as empty, where nothing apart from the ocean and heaven existed. One day God was traveling in his boat when the Devil emerged from the foaming sea and suggested they create the world. The Devil could not construct a world without God's help. He swam to the world's depths and brought sand for God, Who sprinkled it on the ocean to create a world. The world which was birthed was tiny and could not contain God and the Devil. When they inhabited the world, the Devil tried to trick God and push Him off into the deep water while He slept. When God slipped, the world on his side grew the East. The Devil's western half also grew, which ended up in a conflict between him and God. The Creator ascended to the Heavens and pushed the Devil into the abyss – the underworld.

The second myth of the Cosmic Egg begins with absolute darkness. There was an egg in this darkness which held in it the god Svarog. Svarog emerged when the egg was cracked, and there was dust. From this, eggshell grew the divine tree, which divided heaven from the land and sea. The world was put together by gold powder brought by Svarog from the underworld. It represented fire and created life through the sun and the moon. Animals and humans were shaped from the remains of the egg left at the bottom of the shell.

The third myth argues that the world was born from God's body as it was dismembered into different parts of the universe. The sun was born from the deity's radiant face, and the moon was lit by his chest. The auroras, white and vibrant, were born from his eyes, and the stars sprinkled in the night sky emerged from his robe. The wind which gave life to the world was the divine spirit itself. Man was birthed from the bones of God and the soil found on earth. This version appeared in the Dove Book interpreted by the Polish academic Stanislaw Schayer. It contained oral histories of the clergy. According to legend, Tsar David found a book that fell from heaven, and upon reading it, realized it was the history of creation.

While differences between each version persist, there are some common elements; dual deities, darkness and light, the dark underground world, and the heavens. Some legends tell the tale of man's birth when he was created from clay, while the angels were given life by God's sacred light. The dark deity created balance by birthing demons.

Deities

There is no evidence of an organized pantheon within the Slavic faith. The Slavic people did worship deities, but some may be the results of Indo-European influence. These deities may not have been worshiped by everyone across Slavic Europe, and the practices themselves were diverse.

Perun

The most important deity of the Slavs is Perun, who is venerated across Slavic Europe and beyond. He is called Perkunas in Baltic mythology. He is the god of heaven and reigns over thunder and lightning. He is the god of thunder, much like Zeus and Thor in Greek and Norse mythology. His name is derived from the root "per," which means "to strike or hit." He is called Piorun in Polish, meaning "thunder." Perun was venerated throughout the settlements of the Slavs; however, his tale was best recorded in Eastern Slavic resources.

Prince Vladimir the Great is credited in the Ruthenian chronicles with the building of a majestic statue of Perun. He began his rule in the year 980 A.D., and the statues of Slavic deities were placed outside his palace in Kiev. Perun's body was built from wood, while the head was silver with a golden mustache. Since he was the most powerful deity in Slavic myth, he rivaled the Christian God. When the Duke of Kiev converted to Christianity, his statue was annihilated. All the sculptures were ruthlessly destroyed, and signs of Paganism were erased. Perun's statue was disrespected – dragged down by a horse, then beaten and damaged before it was discarded in the river Dnieper. The order was to let his statue float in the vast river, and when it was found ashore, the site was named "Perunja Red" or the "Shallows of Perun."

The expanses of the Slavic region probably had different names for Perun in each region. An instance of these variations is the holy trinity of gods venerated in Rugia, an island where the Slavic tribes of Ruiani (or "Rani") lived in the Middle Ages. The records show that this deity possessed seven visages and seven swords dangling from his waist. His hand held the eighth sword. The other two deities had multiple faces, too, and they were called Porenut and Porevit. Porenut was constructed with four faces and Porevit with five. Porenut had a fifth face which was placed into his chest. "Porevit" literally translates to "the lord of force" and points to his role as the god of military power. Legend also says that Porevit was the son of Perun. A theory suggests that Ruievit is synonymous with Perun reigning over Rugia with his two sons, Porenut and Porevit.

Veles

Veles is second to Perun in importance within Slavic mythology. He is known as the *skotiy bog* in the Ruthenian record, translated to mean that he was the lord of cattle. Since cattle represented wealth and prosperity, he was synonymous with abundance, and so was known as the god of wealth. He has also been linked to the underworld, the deceased, sorcery, poetry, and oath keeping. Some legends describe Verun as the mythical rival of Perun. This points to a common structure within ancient Indo-European legends that records mythical antagonism between two supreme gods. Historians and academics believe that this notion has passed on to post-Christian times and survives within the Slavic creation myth – the opposition between God and Satan. The Devil is another version of Veles. Interestingly, the phrase in Czech folklore, "Jdi za more k Velesu" or "Go across the sea to Veles," translates to "Go to the devil."

Sventovit

The most famous multi-headed deity of Slavic Paganism is Svetovid, also called Sventovit and Svantovit. The Arconians of the Rugia Island worshiped him, and an enormous statue of Svetovid was erected in the center of the temple. Saxo Grammaticus, a Danish historian, observed that the statue possessed four heads and necks, and held a drinking horn in his hand. Svetovid's mustache and hair resemble the fashion of locals. Many forms of war divination were practiced around the building. The divine animal of Svantovit – the white horse – was worshipped there. The horse symbolizes the sea, or Poseidon in Greek mythology, and military strength. His role was akin to that of Triglav and Veles. Gerovit, who is worshipped in Wolgast and Havelberg, is another likely incarnation of Perun. Many Christian chroniclers compared him to Mars, the Roman god of war.

Triglav

Triglav, like Veles, is the god of divination and oaths. The territory of Pomerania or the Baltic Coast is the seat of Triglav. He is considered the local incarnation of Veles. A sculpture of him in Szczecin was described as having his mouth and eyes encased with golden material. This represents the deity's refusal to watch the sins of people. Each head symbolized the three major realms Triglav reined over – the Earth, the underworld, and the heavens.

Some other minor deities are listed below:

- Mokosh - She is one of the few female deities in the pantheon. Some academics argue that her origins can be traced to the legends of Finno-Ugric communities. She also appears in relation to the worshipers of the Great Mother.

- Hors - He is a lunar god, worshiped probably in Kiev in pre-Christian times; he has emerged from the myths of Iran.

- Stribog - He is also known as the god of winds and wealth.

- Svarog - He is the celestial god of the sun, fire, and the blacksmith. He is often compared to the Hephaestus, the Greek deity. Many Western Slavic territories have been named after him, such as Schwerin and Swarzedz.

- Semargl - He was the god of vegetation and good harvest, possibly borrowed from Iranian myths. In Iranian legend, a creature with the body of a dog, called "Simurgh", exists.

- Dazbog - He is the heir of Svarog and is the god of the sun in a fashion akin to his father. He is also the god of divine fire emerging from the earth.

Slavic Paganism contains accounts of demons, house spirits, local gods and goddesses, and lesser deities besides the major deities. *Rod* is essential to the culture and is a symbol of fate in Slavic myth. *Rozhanitsky* are the invisible females who, like the Greek Moirai or the Three Fates, decide a child's destiny after birth. The etymological root of Rod, as well as Rozhanitzy, means "birth" in Slavic. *Dola* is the female goddess who nourishes children and protects the household. She is also called a protective spirit in some versions.

The next concept is that of the Slavic afterlife. Little is known about this concept. Creatures such as vampires, strigoi or *strzyga*, and *upiers* are bloodthirsty demons within Slavic folklore. Strigoi also appear in Romanian mythology and are troubled ghosts who have emerged from the grave. They are shapeshifters with the power to remain invisible and nourish themselves from blood sucked out of their victims. Perhaps these creatures reflect the dark conceptualization of life after death within Slavic Paganism.

Some Slavic mythology asserts that the deceased's spirit travels to the underworld through a magical bridge at night. It was the personification of the Milky Way, and when mortals saw it during the day, it appeared as a rainbow. The Milky Way itself is described as the "Way of the Soul" and the "Way of the Army." The world of the dead was connected to the living via the "Tree of the Family". The *dziady* were the spirits of Slavic ancestors. Slavs attached special value to names. They believed that if the dead man's name is uttered, his identity remains. When people stop taking his name, he merges with the community of nameless spirits. Once these spirits become one nameless force of nature, they shine upon the world of the living as cosmic rays birthed out of the sun.

Nature was mythologized for the Slavs and held ritual importance. For instance, holy trees situated in the cosmos were also Cosmic Mountains. Mountains acted as magical locations, and many Slavic shrines and temples are situated there. Some examples are the Bald Mountain, Sleza, Durmitor or "the Blue Column," and Krivan, which was considered divine by the Slovaks.

Some sources suggest that Slavic gods thirsted for the sensation of animal and human blood. A bishop called John in Mecklenburg is recorded as having his head sacrificed to the gods in 1066. Perun is linked to such sacrifices. While most of these ideas emerge from history written by Christian scribes, there is some speculation that these elements may have existed within Slavic lore. Many cultures in the Indo-European region had elements of human sacrifice.

Horse divination, or the act of gaining knowledge from horses, was a common practice in Slavic cults. They are recorded as white-colored creatures used in rituals of war divination. People observed the behavior of the horse to decide whether a war was lucrative or not.

One of the most experienced academics of the Slavic faith was Aleksander Gieysztorhas, and he noted that the mythological theory incorporates two patterns characteristic of Indo-European folklore. One is the oceanic nature of any being from which all life originates, and the other is the dualistic nature of existence, the product of the partnership of two otherwise oppositional mystical characters.

These characters in the tale told to ethnographers by a nineteenth-century Polish farmer are portrayed as God and the Demon; however, as Gieysztor indicates, those could be terms under which even more prehistoric gods hide – including, maybe, Perun and Veles.

The fundamentally dualistic nature of this story is better understood from Iranian mythology, when we contrast Ahur Mazda and Ariman, and is further clarified by the long-standing strong association between the Slavs and the Iranian tribes like the Sarmatians living in the northern Black Sea zone. As Gieysztor reveals, many significant Slavic religious languages owe these neighborly relations for inspiration, including the symbols of heaven, which is *Nebo* in Slavic and *Nabah* in Iranian, or "god" translated as *Bóg* in the former and *Baga* in the latter.

Modern Slavic Paganism

Slavic Paganism in modernity is called Modern Rodnovery. The religion of the Slavs was reconstructed in the twentieth century. This is attributed to the movement of "Native Slavic Faith" or "Rodnovery." Elements of primordial Slavic religion remain, but they are combined with philosophies of different religions like Hinduism. Rodnover cults mostly perform folk worship and venerate deities on specific days of the year. Some others have constructed a scripture for ritualistic practice, like the Book of the Veles. They combine Hindu Vedas with Slavic mythological practices to form the core of their practice (for instance, the *Maha Vira* of Sylenkoism).

Perhaps because of the ambiguous history of Slavic Paganism, people practice it in diverse ways across the world.

Chapter 9: Indigenous Paganism: A Shamanic View

Shamanism is a supernatural tradition entailing an individual who is supposed to communicate with the spiritual realm through distorted forms of awareness, such as possession. The aim of this is typically to guide these spiritual forces to the real realm to enlist their assistance. In the 19th and 20th centuries, many Western people participating in counter-cultural campaigns developed new magically-religious lucky charms inspired by the beliefs of Pagan cultures from all over the globe, producing what's been called neo-Shamanism. It has resulted in the creation of several Neo-Pagan rituals, all amidst the uproar and allegations of cultural imperialism, misuse, and misappropriation as foreigners have attempted to define and represent communities that they do not affiliate with.

Shamanism is a spiritual tradition and framework. Traditionally, it is mostly connected with aboriginal and native cultures, which embraces the idea that shamans, through a link to some other realm, had the ability to cure the ill, speak with deities, and accompany the deceased to the underworld. It is built around the conviction that spiritual forces such as those in the realm of deities, ghosts, and ancient forces affect our everyday lives.

Given the systemic ramifications of colonization and globalization, which have restricted native communities' freedom to pursue ancestral spirituality, several societies are experiencing a revival because of indigenous self-assertion and the restoration of diverse cultures. These systemic barriers have been resisted by certain communities owing to their detachment from the rest of the world. The nomadic Tuva tribe, whose surviving numbers are currently estimated to be only three thousand, is one example. They are among the most remote groups in Russia; among them, the practice of shamanism has been retained because of their confined nature, enabling their practices to be exempt from the effects of Abrahamic faiths.

Beliefs

Shamanism is centered on the idea that the material universe is permeated by unseen entities or forces that influence people's activities. While the origin of sickness resides in the supernatural world according to traditional beliefs, metaphysical and bodily curing techniques are utilized in synthesis. Typically, the shaman "penetrates the flesh" to tackle the metaphysical affliction and cures by expelling the contagious force.

Most shamans have experience in therapeutic herbs native to their region, and natural therapy is often administered. In certain areas, shamans take guidance from herbs, channeling the plant's influence and curing powers by gaining approval from the innate spirits or guardians. *Curanderos* utilize medicating music called *icaros* to attract spiritual forces in the Peruvian Amazon Basin. A spirit can be invited only if it instructs the shaman about the composition of its rhythm. The usage of totemic artifacts such as stones with unique forces and the essence of animation is quite popular. These traditions are undoubtedly quite old. In Phaedrus, Plato noted how the "first prophecies were the words of an oak" and that the original meaning of the world was revealed in these moments of animation as the people back then found it compelling enough to "listen to an oak or a stone, as long as it was telling the truth."

Belief in witches remains in several cultures, such as the Latin American belief in *brujería*. Many cultures believe that these shamans possess the ability to both heal and destroy. Many with shamanic experience typically possess considerable influence and prominence in society, but they can often be viewed suspiciously or as possibly dangerous. By participating in these customs, a shaman is subjected to considerable physical danger since shamanic herbal ingredients can be harmful or lethal if abused. Spells are widely employed to defend against such threats, and the usage of extremely harmful herbs is strongly institutionalized.

Several tribes in Siberia have shamans who utilize drums. The drum's rhythm helps the shaman enter an enhanced state of mind or trance, or even to embark on a trip across the material and the divine realms. A lot of curiosity surrounds the function performed by the ambiance of the drum on the shaman. The rhythms of the drum affect the space occupied by the shaman as the reverberations allow them to become one with the music's force.

Forms of Shamanism

Siberia & North Asia

Shamanic activity has been regarded as being centered in certain areas, and Siberia is one of them. Many disparate native tribes live in this region, and most of them continue to practice shamanic traditions. Most of the knowledge about shamanism comes from the ethnographic records of Siberian peoples.

With the rise of the rational and scientific modern state, most shamanic cultures have been persecuted, but Manchu Shamanism held an official status during China's Qing dynasty by becoming a subset of the imperial cult, along with other religious cultures such as Taoism and Buddhism. The Forbidden City, situated in Beijing, was the imperial palace of the dynasty, and one of its main halls, known as the Palace of Earthly Tranquility, was dedicated to shamanic activities. The instruments used are still preserved and have become a site of pilgrimage for many.

The definition of a shaman for the Siberian Chukchis people is a person whose body is occupied by a non-earthly force. For them, such a person is divinely ordained and must perform the shaman's function for the good of the people. The Buryats from Mongolia have a practice called *shanar* - it is an event where the shaman picks their replacement by passing their power onto the new shaman. Many groups from Russia who continue to live in isolation still practice shamanism as a living cultural practice, such as the Samoyedic peoples.

With the development of the modern nation-state of the People's Republic of China in 1949, new borders were drawn with Siberia, which Russia ruled at that time. This led to the separation of many tribes from their historical background since they were now confined to Manchuria and Inner Mongolia; such was the case for the nomadic Tungus people, whose culture declined with an incessantly paternalistic state that continued to interfere in their practices.

Native American

There is no one unifying Native American religion or culture since it's a composite term that includes a diverse array of tribes across North America. There are over five hundred and seventy Native American tribes recorded in the USA and about six hundred and thirty-four First Nation groups across Canada. Although their culture has many similarities to shamanism, none of them ever used the word to describe their healers, mystics, singers, and lore-keepers. Just like all the other indigenous cultures across the world, they had their own terms to describe those who performed these important functions within the community.

The authentic representation of Native American and First Nation culture is mostly missing from mainstream academic discourse because of a lack of authentic ethnographic engagement and representation. This is why it's important to take all descriptions of indigenous cultures with a pinch of salt. Most importantly, these practices have been perceived as only existing in the past and having no bearing today, which is a falsification that nominalizes those native communities that continue to practice their beliefs every day.

As opposed to other indigenous groups, most Native American communities do not have specific titles and designations for those who communicate with the spirit world since it's a ritual commonly practiced by all group members on a personal level. The closest that any official religious leader comes to the term "shaman" is the "medicine man," who is regarded as the bridge between the physical and spiritual realms. Medicine barely covers the complexities of the practice since the purpose of such a person is to revitalize the body, connect it to the force and power of nature, and enable the healing of the spirit leading to the healing of the body. Most Native American rituals use the power of a spirit personified as a natural/animalistic force, an ancestor, or even a malevolent entity. What kind of spiritual force could heal a person is determined by the individual circumstances of the patient. For example, an existential malady resulting in sickness could be healed only through reunification with an ancestral spirit. This is significant because, for these peoples, physical sickness was symptomatic of object intrusion or soul loss. The spirits can be considered mere personifications of internal forces that are not visible except through a shaman-like individual.

In the modern era, most indigenous practices are being revitalized across reservations, but years of colonization and genocide have had a detrimental impact on the belief systems of most tribes. The wholesale extinguishing of Native American and First Nation cultures has caused a spiritual and physical decay that these people continue to grapple with.

Mayan and Aztec

The Mayan tradition has its own unique spiritual practices and functionaries who carry out these rituals. These religious leaders have their own hierarchy based on the different duties they perform, which includes praying and sacrificing for the rest of the ethnic group or community. Two gods are considered central, and both are associated with masculinity – Maximón and Martín. These deities belong to the pantheon of the Tz'utujil Mayas of Santiago Atitlán and within this group are priests and brotherhoods specifically dedicated to them. Other than the civic leaders, there are those who are known as seers or "day keepers" who perform the function of shamans. Healing is a performative activity, and so are other priestly duties; all of them require audiences to feed the priest's power, whose characteristics have similarities to shamanism.

The Aztecs of central Mexico have their own religion, including practices such as human sacrifice performed during certain seasons and festivals. Their religion is a polytheistic one, with deities having evolved over the ages as the Aztecs incorporated the gods and goddesses of other religions. The Aztecs are popularly known for their cosmology, which divided the heavens into thirteen realms, with the earth being perceived as made up of nine netherworld layers. Each level is associated with a certain god and has a specific cultural reference in the way it is linked to human life.

The Aztec religion's central god, associated with shamanism, is Tezcatlipoca, which translates to "smoking mirrors." This name is not incidental since it is derived from his connection to obsidian, a material used by early Aztecs to make mirrors. Shamans used obsidian to make prophecies and conduct certain rituals. The shaman would investigate the material's smooth and reflective surface to transpose his gaze back into the past and far into the future. It was essentially a totem used to pass to other realms without being consumed by them. It acted as a mediator between the shaman residing in the earthly realm and the spiritual world.

Aboriginal People of Australia

The Aboriginal people of Australia had an oral tradition whose belief was based on a deification of the earth and a reverence for the "Dreamtime." Dreaming was an essential art that allowed those who sought the past to access it in their dreams – one could go back to the prehistoric time of creation or access the spiritual realm. Many ancestral spirits were revered, such as the Baiame, Dirawong, Rainbow Serpent, and Bunjil. The knowledge that was accessed in Dreaming was incorporated into songs, folklore, legends, and dances, and even today, many aboriginal people continue to use these stories as references for their belief in kinship ties and preserving nature.

Healers were known as *Ngangkari* in certain tribes of central Australia. They were considered to be learned women and men who were revered for their roles as not just curers but also the principal carriers of cultural values and folklores. Most Aboriginal groups did not use the term "shaman" but referred to them as "clever men and women" or *kadji*. *Maban* (or *Mabain*) was a magic material used by these aboriginal shamans to conduct rituals and healing practices. This material was supposed to confer upon the practitioner a spiritual and magical force. Shamans not only ensured that the community lived in harmony with the spiritual entities, but they also conducted ceremonies to initiate others into their cult and even enforce the law of the tribe. Those who broke the tribal law were sentenced by these "clever persons" who used a song to curse the person who broke the law.

Polynesia

One of the main Polynesian tribes is the Māori, who are indigenous to mainland New Zealand. They were settlers who arrived on the island from eastern Polynesia in the 14th century. Their belief system developed independently of other Polynesian cultures and consists of a reverence for nature. They believe that all living things are sacred because of their common descent from *whakapapa*. The central tenet of their culture is the belief that matter possesses within it a life force known as *mauri*. They had personifications for the different aspects of matter, so the ocean was known as *Tangaroa*, *Tāne* was the forest, and *Rongo* represented peace and cultivation.

For these people, certain objects and persons have special significance and contain mana or a powerful essence. The concept of mana as a force of energy in inanimate objects led to the concept of *Tapu* or "sacred restriction" according to which certain objects were not to be touched. These prohibitions were applied to private and public objects, and the rules governing what was considered tapu were ever-shifting.

Any person skilled in a certain task, whether it was praying or hunting, was considered to be a *tohunga*. This concept is similar to shamanism because the tohunga was considered a living spiritual entity that was able to communicate across realms and temporalities. Their rites were specific to the field they practiced and included diverse occupations like linguistics, tattooing, astronomy, canoe building, etc. What made them significant was their knowledge, considered to arrive from the divinities directly to them, and a tohunga was required to pass on their knowledge to a successor. Since much of this knowledge was oral, it has slowly been effaced through the ages.

The island of Papua New Guinea has indigenous tribes that believe that illness and catastrophes are caused by malicious entities known as *masalia*. These forces attach themselves to a person's form and slowly drain them. Shamans perform the important function of revitalizing the affected person by purging these evil forces. They also carry out other significant activities like praying for rain and granting a hunter extraordinary abilities to trap animals.

Chapter 10: Wicca: A Modern Approach

Wicca is a customized practice of ancient witchcraft. The term Wicca is now applied to the modern tradition of Pagan witchcraft and Paganism as a whole. While "witchcraft" and "Wicca" are commonly used synonymously, there are also practices of ancient witchcraft that are not based on Wicca. Wicca was used initially to categorize the practice of witchcraft as a religion. However, popular Western representations also adopted the term to encompass what may previously have been considered natural magic or "white witchcraft." When people refer to themselves as Wiccan, they are usually discussing the sort of religious witchcraft they perform. The media frequently portrays female witches as young girls, but in actuality, witchcraft is performed by men and women of any age. Within modern times, it has become a festival based on nature worship. People who belong to the Wiccan identity engage in rituals based on seasonal festivals like the solstice and equinox. Deities of male and female genders are venerated, and these rituals include herbalism and natural elements. There are moral and ethical laws that govern the Wiccan, and they believe in the afterlife. However, all these practices can differ across sects.

Wicca is a Neo-Pagan faith founded by a British person named Gerald Gardner in the 1940s. Gardner popularized the modern faith with the help of his novels, which were published in 1949, 1954, and 1959. These books are *The Meaning of Witchcraft, High Magic's Aid,* and *Witchcraft Today.* Gardner labeled this Neo-Pagan faith as the "witch cult" and "witchcraft" and named his adherents "the Wica." He also gave them the name "Wicca" (with two 'c's) in his 1959 novel, where the term originated. In Old English, the term means "witch." People who practice Wicca are termed "Wiccans." Before the word "Wicca" was introduced, the faith was often simply named "the craft."

It is currently used as a generic word for several disparate routes that have emerged from Gardner's initial work. These books contain ethics or commandments for behavior and the development of a Wiccan morality. Some Wiccans with primitive lineages may follow laws named "Ardanes." However, many are critical of such laws due to their regressive and outdated nature. Some believe that such laws influence behaviors that are counterproductive to the Wiccan faith. Contemporary scholars like Doreen Valiente argue that such stringent codes were most likely written by Gardner, mimicking primitive language to establish authority over his coven.

Wicca is a modern resurgence of pre-Christian faiths, and some members claim to be part of families directly descended from primitive witches. Wiccans can form groups for practice called covens, or they may practice alone. Mostly, there are multiple ways in which Wiccans perform their faith; however, duotheism, or the worship of two gods of the male and female gender, is common. The male god may be referred to as the "Horned God" and the latter as the "Mother Goddess." People from the unorthodox sect who only believe in a female God are called the "Dianic Wicca." There are polytheistic, pantheistic, and atheistic Wiccans as well. Such Wiccans show respect to deities as a mere symbolic aspect of the religion but do not consider them to actually exist as supernatural beings. The Moon is essential to Wiccans and many holidays revolve around its phases.

Solar equinoxes, solstices, the four natural elements (water, air, fire, earth), and initiation rituals are some other elements celebrated by the religion.

As the primary guide on morality, the Wiccan Rede is at the heart of the religion's spirituality. Etymologically, "rede" translates to "council" or "advice" in ancient German. The main Rede can be translated to, "As ye harm none, do what ye will," and it means "Do what you want to do, but do not harm anything in the process." This signifies the basic tenets of the Wicca – to act fairly and ensure everyone's wellbeing around you. The thought that actions have larger consequences than oneself is connected to the idea of nature as well. Coexistence is a primary philosophy – humans exist with the natural elements around them, which must be respected equally.

A significant law among Wiccans is "The Rule of Threefold Return." This law is similar to Hindu karmic theory and argues that your action will return to you three times more than what you originally planned, so if you act with bad intentions, you will suffer. A proper Wiccan must focus on doing good things to avoid suffering in life. This rule of the "threefold" is ritually revealed to initiates during the second stage of induction. The ritual consists of the initiator whipping the initiate, and the former returns the action three times on the initiator that whipped them. This rule was published in Gerald Gardner's book *High Magic Aid*. Another Wiccan called Raymond Buckland produced a different definition of the Rule of Threefold Return in 1986. He clarified the karmic content of this law and argued that it is not merely a Wiccan code of conduct. He attached a larger significance to actions by placing them in a supernatural realm of justice.

The performance of rituals may be conducted in specific places of worship and magic, which are called altars. When Wiccan practice was limited to covens, there was a single altar for coven gatherings. However, with the rise of individual practitioners, altars began to be built for personal use. The common objects of spiritual significance used for Wiccan practices are as follows:

Athame

This is a mystical knife utilized in ceremonies. Customarily, the athame has a black painted handle. Its use is never to sever some material; instead, it's used to create a 'cut' in the shape of a circle into the air to project a magic circle. In the rituals of "wine and cakes" and the "great rite," the atham symbolizes the male organ.

Chalice

It is a motif of the female vagina and is used for the "wine and cakes ritual" and the "great rite" ritual.

Pentacle

The Wiccan pentacle is a solid disk the width of a tiny saucer with a pentagram inscribed within the perimeter. The Wiccan pentacle may be constructed of various materials like wood, metal, or ceramic. In Wiccan rites, the pentacle profile can be seen in the fourfold cardinal points (west, south, north, and east) which expose the talisman to the "deities of the watchtowers" that are thought to exist in specific directions.

Wand

A wand's function is to give direction to mystical energy. It is a long stick – stretching from your elbow to the wrist, traditionally – used for ritual practice. It can be adorned with ribbons, wire, crystals, or paint.

These objects are generally placed inside the altar, including a besom (naturally-produced broom of ancient design), candles, statues of gods and goddesses, or incense sticks. The broom is particularly significant as it has the power to "sweep" the negative spirits or energies away. It is also a symbol of witchcraft in the contemporary representation of witches in popular culture.

For individual or solitary altars, the objects are derived from collective Wiccan rituals. Gardner named them "working tools," and they are as follow:

- Black-handled knife or Athame
- Sword called "magical sword"
- Bowl of water
- Bowl of asperger
- Bowl of salt
- White-handed knife or "Bolline"
- Candles
- Pentacle
- A bell
- Container for burning incense (censer)
- A whip with multiple cords (scourge)
- Binding cords

Wiccan Holidays

There are two major Wiccan festivals: "esbats" and "sabbats". There are thirteen full- moon esbats and the cycle of eight sabbats. The former takes place when the moon is full, and the latter at intervals within the "wheel of the year."

The Wheel of the Year is a periodic cycle of annual festivals (occurring seasonally) practiced by many western Pagans and composed of the year's major solar cycles and their midpoints. Though each festivals' terms differ from one Pagan practice to another, syncretic associations generate a commonality of reference, especially in Wicca, to all the festivals that relate to solar events which occur quarterly by the calendar as "quarter days" and the events in-between as "cross-quarter days". The various groups of modern Paganism often differ as to each festival's exact date, depending on variations such as the phase of the moon and the geographical hemisphere location.

Monitoring the seasonal cycle was essential to several peoples, both ancient and modern. New Pagan festivals that depend on the Wheel of the Year focus on folk customs, independent of real historical practices. To Wiccans, each holiday is often alluded to as the Sabbat, based on Gerald Gardner's argument that when the Jewish term "Shabbat" was merged with the rhetoric of heretical celebrities, this word was transmitted down from the Middle Ages.

In certain beliefs of western Pagan cosmology, all occurrences are known to be cyclical, with time as a continuous period of development and withdrawal connected to the periodic death and resurrection of the Sun. This loop is often used as a micro-and-macrocosm of several life cycles in a tremendous sequence of Universe cycles. Customarily, the periods that fall on the annual period's landmarks represent the start and the center of the four major seasons. They are thought to be important and are also the venue for big community festivals. These eight events are the most popular period for cultural festivities.

Even though the "major" holidays are typically quarter-days and cross-quarter-days, some festivals are often celebrated during the year, particularly among non-Wiccan practices such as polytheistic restoration associations and in keeping with other indigenous customs.

In Wicca and rituals influenced by it, gatherings related to solar trends have traditionally been immersed in solar myths and meaning based on the light's life cycles. Such synchronization with nature links witchcraft closely to the essence of nature. Likewise, the Wiccan esbats are historically related to the celestial cycles. Together they reflect the most popular celebrations of Wiccan-influenced types of Neo-Paganism, particularly in modern Witchcraft communities.

Another important ritual is the Wiccan Funerary Rite. Each funeral can differ from sect to coven, yet they share some features, especially the principle of ensuring environmentally-conscientious burials are conducted. The dead person is laid to rest in a natural atmosphere, wrapped in a shroud made of organic cloth to allow natural and quick decomposition. The earth's divinity is respected by the body's return to it and the nutrition it provides for new life forms to grow through death. Sometimes burial outside or in a natural setting is not permitted by law. Wiccans may bury the ashes after cremation in such a case. There are special ways of honoring the dead, such as memorializing them by distributing some ashes to loved ones. This allows for different ways of remembrance.

Wiccans believe in the afterlife that leads to reincarnation. When someone dies, their spirit lives on by being birthed as a new person. It is believed that these reincarnated souls have a chance to meet their friends and family of previous lives. Death is not seen as salvation from the earth. Reincarnation symbolizes the pleasure a person can achieve by being born multiple times on earth. The experience of life itself is the gift. Living is related to learning and gathering knowledge; however, there is a world beyond constant reincarnation, called "Summerland." This supernatural place is also known as the "Land of Youth," and is where spirits seek salvation once they have completed the cycle of death and reincarnation. It is the realm of joy, bliss, and ultimate transcendence. It is imagined as a place with immense greenery, abundant in beauty and peace. Spirits may also rest here to reconnect with those they have lost.

The funeral service itself is an expression of respect for the deceased person's wishes. There may be rules which disallow non-Wiccans from participating in the ceremony. In contemporary times, relatives and close ones are generally allowed to be a part of the final farewell. The service is divided into two parts - the funeral ritual and the burial of the body. The funeral ritual is presided over by a Priest or a Priestess who directs the ceremony with the ushers' or assistants' help. The altar is used for laying down the body, and the ritual setting is cleared of all other objects. The place is made fit for rituals by the Priestess, and the attendees wait outside the sacred circle. Incantations and spiritual chants serve as forces of magic. Speaking is essential; mourners and Priests may address the deceased and express parting sentiments for their journey into the afterlife. The next part of the funeral is the burial. The body is made fit for burial by the direction of the Priestess. After the burial is complete, all are invited to recall precious memories with the deceased and pray for their peaceful rest. All these rituals of sharing and expressed intimacy are a means to maintain the strength offered by the community. There may be specific prayers and ritual chants that can be found on Wiccan coven resources and sites for reference.

Wiccan philosophies and rituals have been adopted by the "Goddess Spirituality Movement." This movement is primarily based on celebrating anti-patriarchal gods. The community consists of people who have abandoned the idea of a male supreme deity. The Goddess is female, and her femininity is divine and supreme.

Wicca also shares similarities with Druidry. As already noted, like Wicca, Druidry is based on a connection with nature through outdoor settings and also considers the environment as being divine. Their rituals are deeply embedded in sustaining and seeking further connection with an all-powerful nature. The Druids and Wiccans see themselves as the guardians of the earth and stress its conservation. However, Wicca is not as Celtic as Druidry. Magic or sorcery is seminal to the Wiccan tradition, unlike Druidry. Artistic expressions like poetry, music, and performance are considered fertile paths for spiritual rejuvenation.

One salient principle central to a Wiccan lifestyle is that it offers an autonomy of faith-practice by maintaining the legitimacy of diverse practices. Wiccans believe in consequentialism, as illustrated by ethical and moral supernatural laws. The belief in actions loaded with karmic consequences fosters a sense of empathy. Such principles offer a legitimate counter to false ideas about witchcraft as something evil and dark. Traditionally, witches have been seen as dangerous and unreliable. However, the resurgence of Wicca has allowed for a new way of experiencing faith. The neo-Wiccan academia has allowed for women's empowerment by stressing the strength of the feminine form. In 2002, a research project called "Enchanted Feminism: The Reclaiming Witches of San Francisco" has shown that some Wiccans were members of the second wave of feminism. North America is a good place to study the prevailing ideas of feminism within Neo-Pagan religious groups. As a religious movement, Wicca has become intermeshed with larger political struggles and has provided an alternate lifestyle of activism and care for its members.

Chapter 11: Agnostic Paganism & Other Paths

Humanistic or secular Paganism is an approach that embraces the values and ideals of Paganism while retaining a progressive viewpoint. Techniques of secular Paganism differ, but they always inculcate reverence for all life forms and the world itself while dismissing faith in gods. Secular Pagans tend to acknowledge deities as helpful symbols for various life stages or even portray rituals as solely mental activities. The 18th century created a substantial volume of study that attempted to reveal ideas from the medieval period, particularly Pagan myths and deities, as mere constructs of the mind. This led directly to positivist and atheistic conceptualizations of classical mystical ideas.

History of Agnostic & Atheistic Paganism

A common allegation towards Pagans who don't believe in gods by certain polytheistic Pagans is that they misuse the term "Pagan." Traditional Paganism, they claim, was associated with polytheism, and so modern Paganism must also be polytheistic. Naturalistic and humanist Pagans seem to be much more forward-looking, avoiding the pitfalls of scavenging the past. Unlike Paganism styles that aim to recreate the beliefs of ancestral Pagans through recovered texts, naturalistic and humanist Pagans have mostly resisted efforts to justify their practices through constant references to history. For them, the importance of spiritual life rests in its relevance to the community that exists in the now.

The claim that secular Pagans misuse the word "Pagan" often disregards the reality that there were agnostics and other non-theists in pagan history. Preceding the logical thinkers of the 20th century who would clarify the roots of spirituality as the human determination to make a mystical reality knowable, Xenophanes of Colophon in the 5th century B.C. proposed that the deities were reflections of human attributes. Xenophanes's major concern was "God" (in the singular), yet this "God" was more or less associated with the essence or logical structure of the cosmos rather than some spiritual entity.

Other naturalistic thinkers followed. The first to be prosecuted for heresy because of his skepticism was Anaxagoras. Hippo of Samos was the first to claim that the spirit was little other than the consciousness of the person. Likewise, the idea that the soul was composed of atoms and distributed after death was promulgated by Democritus. An important moment in history was the composition of Thucydides' biography that refused to appeal to divine forces, the first of its kind.

Some or more of these people may well have been alluded to as *atheoi* (atheist), but they certainly did not reference themselves in this manner. In reality, the earliest allusions to the atheoi are not those who distrusted the deities, but those who were discarded by the deities – those who existed outside the deities' hegemonic structure. The Epicureans, for instance, were generally called the Atheoi. Although they continued to believe in the deities and opposed such a classification, they disagreed that the deities had created the cosmos or that they participated in the creation of the universe. They also claimed that praying to the deities did not affect them. Their deities were virtually insignificant to them, save for their rare presence in visions.

Other Pagan thinkers, though they did not call themselves skeptics, often pursued metaphorical outlooks on legends, viewing the deities as symbols for natural events or personal characteristics. For instance, Theagenes of Rhegium connected water with Poseidon, Hephaestus and Apollo with fire, wind with Hera, lust with Aphrodite, Athena with wisdom, Ares with clamor, and so on. The theory that prehistoric men had venerated all objects which were helpful to humanity, so Demeter was associated with bread and Dionysus with wine, was put forth by Prodicus of Ceos. Later on, the Stoics such as Chrysippus, Cleanthes, and Zeno, often connected various deities with particular objects and attributes.

Many contemporary Paganism practitioners have established humanistic, agnostic, or atheistic methods in which essential elements of Pagan beliefs are accepted, but gods are not worshiped as actual or divine entities. These methods take a number of methodological approaches.

Naturalist Paganism

Naturalistic Pagans believe in a diversity of ideologies and might choose to be animists, atheists, or even pantheists. Most of them don't tend to use theistic terminology, but some continue to do so. The use of such language by people who don't identify as theists might be confounding to some, but many use such terminology because they believe words have powers. Without the use of sacred language, they reason, they won't be able to truly immerse themselves in the universe's spiritual nature. The power of language in religion is important, even if the actual worldview does not coincide with the words' ideological connotations. B. T. Newberg notes: "*The imagination must be captivated and transformed by a vision, not of what one is not, but of what one is or could be. This missing element may be embodied in symbols that remind, invite, and inspire. The individual must be able to interact imaginatively with the symbols in ritual or meditation and fill them up as they were with experience and affect. At that point, when they are charged with personal meaning and emotion, they may become powerful motivators of thought and behavior. They radiate the power to transform."*

The use of such language is always in flux, and those words which will be used during a ritual are determined by the nature of the practice itself. The context sets the language, since most Pagans continue to believe that forces beyond us exist and determine our thinking even if they aren't necessarily anthropomorphic deities (the projection of human attributes onto nature). Since the words "god" or "gods" always signify certain spiritual powers, especially subconsciously, it is difficult to disregard the power of such charged terminology. These words carry with them ancestral and spiritual associations that have powerful emotive effects and can allow one to access altered states of mind. Most Naturalist Pagans don't believe there is a God but just try to home in on the emotional force embedded within the word.

Animistic language is helpful to Naturalist Pagans since it affects unique areas of the mind not accessible to non-animistic language. The animistic expression appears to stimulate the areas of the mind correlated with human society and interconnection, as compared to the portion of the mind that organizes things and abstract ideas. So, we grow responsive to a form of interaction with nature that might have been unlikely had we used more rational vocabulary, and we become more prone to transformational theological encounters that arise from that interaction.

Technopaganism

Technopaganism is the usage of electronic technologies or songs in the context of Neo-Paganistic practices. This could involve swapping conventional supernatural equipment with machines, such as utilizing the microwave as a hearth, having a "Drive of Shadows" instead of the "Book of Shadows," and utilizing a light marker as a wand. In many other activities, electronics enhance the focus of mystical practices such as using rocks and spells lending efficiency to ordinary artifacts or digital characters in games. Western and modern cultural trends, such as urban shamanism and psychedelic raves, are related to technopaganism. It deals with the mystical and supernatural elements of technological and scientific culture.

Related to this is the usage of electronic symbols to explain metaphysical events and mainstream imagery in religious settings. If applied to explain structures of religion, technopaganism centers on the metaphysical dimensions of networks. This could involve the idea that artificial objects and things of everyday life, such as houses, highways, vehicles, and others, have their own essence or totem forces. It also applies to larger objects like towns. One assumption that has created a significant debate still ongoing is whether or not the Internet has a special essence.

Jungian Polytheism

Jungian polytheism is a component of the Pagan tradition that situates the supernatural within the self; having the spiritual reside in yourself doesn't imply sanctifying your self-conscious ego - that would mean being delirious. What we deem as being "me" or "the self" is far bigger than the human mind — which is only the visible tip of the iceberg. The "self" involves a subconscious much "larger" than what we normally conceive of as "the self." This is the theory of the psychoanalyst Carl Jung.

What is essential for this dialogue is recognizing that this subconscious identity is not a single unified one. It is composed of a multitude of fragmented identities in the backdrop of the active and thinking self. These incomplete selfhoods are not created; they are found through things like therapy, hallucinations, and psychoanalytical study.

When these fragmented parts are left uncontrolled they force us towards destruction, since they're all competing for supremacy. At every specified instant, we can be "captured" by one of those identities that steers us or "drives" us. Through making space for each of these entities in our waking existence, a special period and a holy rite to respect each of them in their own way, we add balance to the turmoil that is the "I." It can be achieved by counseling or in several other forms. Pagans instead use rites and prayers. The aim of the practice is not the dominance of these fragmented parts but inner peace; by using ceremonies, we can merge these fragmented parts within ourselves. Personal strength derives from putting all these conflicting unconscious powers into a kind of equilibrium.

But why do we label them as deities? The rationale for why we name them "deities" is that no other term accurately explains the immense impact these forces have on our existence. They're residing in and driving us in a literal way. They decide our destiny and how a deity might do it. We may even term them devils, but the intention is to sanctify them, not to vilify them; to respect them, and regard each of them as sacred. Upholding these "deities" will have the same impact that so many others achieve through conventional religious practices, such as gaining spiritual regeneration and transformational powers.

Convent of Unitarian Universalist Pagans

Known through the acronym CUUP, it is a group of Unitarian Universalists who believe in the tenets of traditional and modern Paganism, such as the cyclical nature of time and the reverence of the seasons of nature. CUUP helps people develop Pagan practices by experimenting with different forms of rituals such as music, dance, poetry, and visual arts.

The convent is a Pagan offshoot of the larger Unitarian Universalist ideology, which believes in helping its members search for meaning in the world without asserting any kind of dogma or belief that they must subscribe to. The organization's purpose is the spiritual and personal growth of its members regardless of the form of deities they believe in. CUUP is focused far more on praxis-based activities to enhance spiritual unification, and carries out various practices to preserve the earth, and donates to different organizations that help sustain the principles it believes in.

The main principles of CUUP are open so they can be revised and rewritten depending on the wants and needs of its members. This allows for a more democratic process of a religious organization that ensures an inclusive form of membership. The main values of CUUP are intellectual freedom and mutual empathy for all living things. Many members are atheists and agnostics, while others continue to believe in traditional deities.

Chapter 12: The Modern Pagan: Choose the Right Path for You

Among the multiple Pagan religions that exist, you can choose any path that fits your purpose. You can become a Wiccan, a Hindu, an Agnostic Pagan, or follow any other faith you like. You just have to ensure that the religion you choose is suitable for your personality and future. The point of faith is to give direction to your daily life and provide peace to your psyche. This chapter will cover specific tips and tricks to help you determine which sect is perfect for you.

Answer these questions based on the core beliefs of Paganism to figure out a direction for your belief:

- Do you feel close to nature and wish to protect it?
- Do you believe in the cycle of birth, death, and rebirth?
- Are you sensitive to the consequences of your actions?
- Do you believe in individual moral and ethical freedom to attain peace?

- Are you empathetic to the suffering of animate as well as inanimate beings?
- Are you open to believing in multiple deities or one absolute God?
- Have you always been fascinated by magic as a lifestyle?
- Are you simply curious about the diverse faiths in existence?
- Do you want to gain exposure to different cultural practices for research purposes?

If your answer to most of these questions is "yes," you agree with some fundamental beliefs of Paganism. If you are more inclined to the last two questions, you may want to become an expert or study Paganism academically. You will need to build a practical plan if you want to be a modern practitioner of Paganism.

The first step is to be specific. Avoid reading too many random sources on the internet without planning the path you want to follow. A good strategy is to research particular concepts like Wiccan rituals and Pagan traditions. Ask yourself what you are attracted to; Neo-Druidism, Shamanism, Asatru, or Green Witchcraft? Think deeply about what ideologies you have and how they match with each Pagan tradition. For example, if you care about environmental conservation and women's rights, the Neo-Wiccan or Green Witchcraft can offer you a chance to flourish. You might be an academic interested in learning about the different cultural impacts of Paganism; if that is your goal, begin streamlining your research.

A tip for researching is to find basic facts on religion and learn about its core beliefs. This will also help you in sieving through the myths and misconceptions attached to contemporary Paganism. You must make sure your decision is based on a realistic idea of what it means to be a Wiccan or Neo-Pagan. Additionally, you must research all the Pagan beliefs, history, specific religious movements, influences, and transformations over the centuries. This will help you to make a final decision on what enamors you. You can also choose to follow multiple outlooks.

Most Pagan faiths have a process of initiation. Find out how to become a part of a coven or a community and coach yourself on specifics. You may feel uncomfortable or overwhelmed if you are unaware of the sacrifices and actions you need to take up. For instance, if you want to be a Druid, you need to go through a structured initiation process. You cannot simply initiate yourself. There are levels of achievement and criteria that must be met for your successful membership; however, you can also choose to follow an individual path and become a solitary Pagan.

If you are still confused, read your sources closely. Pick up more books and do a close reading of each aspect. Ask yourself - does this make sense to you? Do you think it's ridiculous to believe in a certain aspect of the faith? Are you unclear about the topic? When you list out your fears and apprehensions, you will be able to engage in introspection better. Think about the author of the book - do you relate to them? Faith is deeply personal, and you need to make sure you relate to the community you want to join.

A great tip is to prepare a list of pros and cons. Take a piece of paper, divide it into two parts - on the left side, list pros, and use the right side to list cons. When you translate your conflicts on paper, you get a visual look into your thoughts. Having these ideas side by side will help you figure out the stakes involved in each benefit or potential harm.

You need to get a real picture of your desire to follow a certain path. You can go to the public library to read specific books. Thrift stores with second-hand books are also a good place to find specific books for study. The internet is another resource that you can use to your advantage. Make sure the online resources you are referring to are legitimate and well-researched. Read book reviews and follow community threads to figure out which authors you like. Once you have built a library for yourself, you can refer to it for clarity whenever you wish. If you are still unsure about the reading list, check out study guides for beginners on sites dedicated to Paganism. It is impossible to read everything, and therefore, you should do a strategic reading. Some books might be metaphysical with tough terms and ideas. You need to spend time - develop a solid base for your intellectual concerns. Noting down arguments that interest you - whether you agree with them or not - is a method to compile your thought process in one place.

Such research will help you discover networks that will connect you to covens or groups. People who actually practice faith are the best resource for understanding the lifestyle of a Pagan. Finding folks with similar ideologies will help you discover a community of people and realize what you want for yourself. You can join a Meetup or go to local Spiritual stores and interact with people there. They can guide you to legitimate information. Even if you want to be a solitary practitioner, you can still approach people to brainstorm with them. Online chats and support groups can help you talk to real sorcerers and experienced magic practitioners.

The next step is to figure out whether you want to be a Solitary Wiccan or a Pagan. You may be restricted by geography or personal reasons from joining a coven, or you may simply wish to remain solitary.

Eclectic Paganism

Once you have followed these steps, you might be interested in practicing Eclectic Paganism. It is a branch of Wicca which allows you to forge your own beliefs and philosophies. As a part of the Neo-Wiccan tradition, it does not have to fit into particular definitions. You can follow this path as a Solitary Wiccan or join a coven that ascribes to the Eclectic vision. This will be the correct path for you if you do not want to follow stringent practices that restrict your individuality. Eclectics mix parts of Paganism with different religions and metaphysical schools of thought. As Melissa Harrington wrote in her book *Handbook of New Age*, "Eclectic Pagans do not follow any particular Paganism, but follow a Pagan religious path that includes the overall Pagan ethos of reverence for the ancient gods, participation in a magical world view, stewardship and caring for the Earth, and nature religion."

As modern Pagans, Eclectics often use social media to forge communities and interact with people across borders. When the faith in question falls within a minority, social media acts as a safe space for discussion, interaction, and learning. Many Pagan communities thrive and come together purely through social media. Like oral traditions, information reaches people through the internet in this age. In the past covens, communities, and families learned of indigenous practices through the generational oral transmission of information.

While Eclectic Paganism is a non-concrete, liberal path for many, it has been accused of cultural appropriation since it does not account for lines between faiths and traditions. Communities whose practices are adopted rarely appreciate the misappropriation of their culture. The multiplicity can create phenomena such as the "witchy aesthetic" and render faith a mere fashion trend or commodity. Many followers believe that this is disrespectful towards the faith; however, as an Eclectic, you can make sure you are conscious of your actions through research and communication with experts around you.

Some paths other than Eclectic Paganism are listed below:

Folklore

Such Paganism is focused on mythologies, oral histories, legends, epics, fairy tales, and customs. The knowledge contained in folklores will help you differentiate between ancient and contemporary practices.

Occult

You can follow this path if you want to seek knowledge that is forbidden or concealed from general access. People often associate such practices with dark magic relating to death and evil spirits.

Historic

Such practice will propel you on a historical journey. You can access archives, study ancient beliefs and practices through archaeology, music, literature, and art. You can delve into specific pantheons or communities which worship one deity.

Syncretism

This is a mixture of Pagan and Non-Pagan beliefs. It often blurs the lines between different influences and offers a non-strict path. If you are not interested in being tied down by one ideology, this might be suitable for you.

Self-Dedication

If you wish, you can dedicate yourself as a Modern Pagan. This can be done by a process called self-dedication. Since initiation requires the approval of an individual or a group, this ritual will help you remain dedicated without rites of initiation. This will motivate you for the rest of your journey and make you feel connected to the energies you have been seeking.

Remember that this ritual is not informal. It holds immense ritual importance, and most people pick auspicious or specific days for it. For example, you should only do this ritual once you believe that you have studied and understood your chosen faith. Most people do it after one year and one day of completing their practice. Others choose the night of a New Moon as it symbolizes fresh beginnings. Before the actual ritual, you should take a bath with salts, incantations, and meditation as a purificatory rite. You can choose to prepare an altar with objects of ritual importance, and you can craft them yourself. Remember that this ritual should not be practiced randomly. Some people choose new names to present themselves to the deities. The point is to open up your spiritual path and establish yourself as a metaphysically connected devotee. Memorizing your ritual is another tip. Plan what you want to say to the gods throughout the ceremony.

Maintain a Pagan journal and note down spiritual thoughts and philosophies to guide you.

Remember that by self-dedicating, you are creating a new identity for yourself. Your life will change forever, and you will feel reborn. This ritual aims to make you feel confident and comfortable with your identity as a Pagan.

Some objects you will need are - salt, a white candle, and blessing oil.

Begin by sprinkling some salt around you and stand on it. When you light the candle, imagine its heat on your face, and let the warmth enter your body. Light is symbolic of ancient powers and energies. Concentrate on the bright flame and repeat your spiritual purpose internally. Remember what motivates you and nudge yourself to imagine why this path is important to you. For example, you can say, *"I have been birthed by the gods, and I seek their blessing."* You can simply dip your hand in the blessing oil and use it for anointing your forehead or trace a pentagon on your skin. Its nourishment will keep you calm and help you absorb the blessings of the deities. Keep anointing your lips, chest, heart, hands, and so on and articulating the blessings you want to seek. Some Pagans follow this technique; however, you can seek guidance from a practicing coven member or solitary.

Apart from a self-dedication ritual, you can also learn some basic magic. Many Pagans believe in magic as an occurrence of daily life, while others may not use it. If you are interested in practicing Pagan magic, look into the following types of magic and decide what suits you best:

Magic Herbalism

It is used for the healing and rejuvenation of the body. It is also connected to lore. People practicing herbalism tap into indigenous knowledge systems from pre-existing written text transmitted by oral tradition. Like the useful properties of rare plants and their impact on the body and psychology, deep knowledge of nature is part of magic herbalism.

Magical Oils

Anointing is an important ritual, and you can find oils made of various kinds of herbs to use in rituals. They have aromatic, healing, and magical properties that you can research. You can make your oils by mixing different elements and learning basic oil-making techniques. You can refer to Wiccan practice texts.

Poppet Magic

Poppet is another term for a doll, and this is the most traditional type of magic. You need to imagine the poppet as the person you want to practice magic on. Creating the doll in the image of the individual will help you focus your magical energies. You can create your poppets for specific purposes.

Candle Magic

The easiest way to cast a spell is by using candle magic. It is a simple but powerful tool and does not require any other extravagant objects. The flame of the candle carries power in itself, and you can use it to direct your energies into the spell.

Magical Crystals

There are nineteen major magical crystals, each of which has unique mystical properties. The choice of the crystal depends on the intention of the spell you want to cast. For example, obsidian is used to detoxify the body as it originates from a volcanic eruption. It symbolizes fire and is used for intuition, unraveling the subconscious, and scrying. Similarly, you can find which of the nineteen stones are most suitable for you: Moonstone, Zircon, Tiger's Eye, Quartz, Turquoise, Sapphire, Obsidian, Lapiz Lazuli, Opal, Jade, Garnet, Jasper, Hematite, Diamond, Amethyst, Carnelian, Bloodstone, Agate, and Amber.

You can follow the resources mentioned below if you are confused by the abundance of information on each path:

- The Gylden Foundation
- Children of Artemis
- Order of Bards, Ovates, and Druids
- Asatru UK
- The Druid Network
- The UK Pagan Council
- British Druid Order

Ultimately, only you can decide the right path for yourself. This is no set guide for following Paganism – you need to embrace the diversity of the faith. Channel your spiritual energies throughout your journey, communicate with your inner self, and practice regularly. Faith is a lifestyle and an intimate part of who you are. Make sure the path you choose is in tandem with your most authentic self. You are a creature of change and movement – embrace it.

Conclusion

Now you know about multiple Pagan religions, from Hellenic practices to Neo-Pagan movements like Heathenism. Learning about any religion can be challenging, as there are diverse elements involved in each practice. This book has highlighted the historical, philosophical, and practical aspects of the major types of Paganism. If you want to become a practicing Wiccan or are simply seeking more knowledge on the subject, this book will have provided you with tips and tricks to master the topic of Paganism.

These suggestions come with guidelines to kick start your progress. The last chapter has helped you identify the resources and methods for additional research and will guide you on how to get in touch with real communities to help you on your journey. This book presented difficult concepts using short and precise explanations, so you do not have to spend countless hours reading.

The information provided will act as a holistic guide for your spiritual development. Refer to its chapters closely whenever you feel lost on your path to Paganism.

Good luck, and thank you for purchasing this book!

Here's another book by Mari Silva that you might like

Your Free Gift (only available for a limited time)

Thanks for getting this book! If you want to learn more about various spirituality topics, then join Mari Silva's community and get a free guided meditation MP3 for awakening your third eye. This guided meditation mp3 is designed to open and strengthen ones third eye so you can experience a higher state of consciousness. Simply visit the link below the image to get started.

https://spiritualityspot.com/meditation

References

Basic Paganism Beliefs: What DO Pagans Believe? (2019, February 18). Otherworldly Oracle.

https://otherworldlyoracle.com/basic-paganism-beliefs-what-do-pagans-believe/

BBC - Religions - Paganism: History of modern Paganism. (2002, October 2). Www.Bbc.co.uk.

https://www.bbc.co.uk/religion/religions/paganism/history/modern_1.shtml

Celtic religion - Beliefs, practices, and institutions. (2019). In Encyclopædia Britannica.

https://www.britannica.com/topic/Celtic-religion/Beliefs-practices-and-institutions

Glinski, M. (2016). What Is Known About Slavic Mythology. Culture.Pl. https://culture.pl/en/article/what-is-known-about-slavic-mythology

Heathenry (new religious movement). (2017). Asuscomm.com.

http://wilearncap.asuscomm.com:81/wikipedia_en_all_novid_2017-08/A/Heathenry_(new_religious_movement).html

Hellenism – The Pagan Federation. (n.d.). https://www.paganfed.org/hellenism/

Lesson Three ~ The Gods and Goddesses. (n.d.). The Druid Network. https://druidnetwork.org/what-is-druidry/learning-resources/polytheist/lesson-three/

Odinism. (n.d.). Odinism and Asatru: Basic Facts. https://www.odinism.net/

Paganism | religion. (n.d.). Encyclopedia Britannica. https://www.britannica.com/topic/paganism

Paganism and Rome. (2019). Uchicago.Edu.

https://penelope.uchicago.edu/~grout/encyclopaedia_romana/greece/paganism/paganism.html

Paganism | World Library - eBooks | Read eBooks online. (n.d.). Www.Worldlibrary.In.

http://www.worldlibrary.in/articles/eng/Paganism

Patnaik, D. (2019, August 12). Equating Paganism With Hinduism. Devdutt. https://devdutt.com/articles/equating-

paganism-with-hinduism/

Roman religion - The imperial epoch: the final forms of Roman paganism. (n.d.). Encyclopedia Britannica. https://www.britannica.com/topic/Roman-religion/The-imperial-epoch-the-final-forms-of-Roman-paganism

What is Paganism? - Pagan Federation International. (2011). Pagan Federation International.

https://www.paganfederation.org/what-is-paganism/

Who are Pagans? The History and Beliefs of Paganism. (2019, September 23). Christianity.com; Salem Web Network. https://www.christianity.com/wiki/cults-and-other-religions/pagans-history-and-beliefs-of-paganism.html

Wiginton, P. (2019, July 6). What is the Asatru Pagan Tradition? Learn Religions.

https://www.learnreligions.com/asatru-modern-paganism-2562545

Printed in Great Britain
by Amazon